IN PURSUIT OF WILD EDIBLES

IN PURSUIT OF WILD EDIBLES

A Forager's Tour

JEFFREY GREENE

UNIVERSITY OF VIRGINIA PRESS

CHARLOTTESVILLE & LONDON

University of Virginia Press

Printed in the United States of America on acid-free paper

First published 2016
First paperback edition published 2017
ISBN 978-0-8139-4100-4 (paper)
1 3 5 7 9 8 6 4 2

The Library of Congress has cataloged the hardcover edition as follows:
Library of Congress Cataloging-in-Publication Data
Names: Greene, Jeffrey, 1952– author.
Title: In pursuit of wild edibles : a forager's tour / Jeffrey Greene.
Description: Charlottesville : University of Virginia Press, [2016] |
Includes bibliographical references and index.
Identifiers: LCCN 2015037817 | ISBN 9780813938578 (cloth : alk. paper) |
ISBN 9780813938585 (ebook)
Subjects: LCSH: Wild foods—Europe. | Greene, Jeffrey, 1952– —Travel—
Europe. | Sustainable living. | Cooking (Wild foods). | LCGFT: Cookbooks.
Classification: LCC TX360.E8 G74 2016 | DDC 641.3/03—dc23
LC record available at http://lccn.loc.gov/2015037817

For my father, Joseph E. Greene,
and Mary

Contents

Preface

CURIOUS GOATS will nibble anything, they say, and go to acrobatic extremes to do it. They'll clamber onto the roof of your car if it helps them tug the leaves off a willow or almost any other type of tree, for that matter. They do vanishing tricks in orchards and gardens, especially when they find saplings or rose bushes. They will even romp through unattended laundry hung in a breeze.

Goats appear at the earliest cusp of my memory, alert creatures of my emerging consciousness. I grew up drinking goat's milk, and I still remember the kids perched atop the small fieldstones where our fencing marked the Connecticut–New York State borderline otherwise indistinguishable in the woods. Goats can stand four feet on a pebble, as my mother loves to say even now.

These goats were Nubians, and yet they could fly, casually springing several feet off the ground whenever they took it into their heads to do so. Standing on their hind legs, they were tall enough to lick my father's face. In the winter when he came in from feeding them, he'd smell of hay and cold as he stomped off snow in the entryway of our four-room house, which seemed forever in a state of repair.

On occasion our goats ate mountain laurel, poison for them and humans, and memories of their awful writhing color what I learned later: it can be hard to save goats from themselves. Obviously, it's the same with us, if we are not prudent. Plants are ingeniously toxic and incidentally medicinal; they release odors to communicate with the animals of the world. Mountain laurel, the Connecticut state flower, contains cyanide, and one of our big black mother goats died from eating it. My father buried her under some of the dirt and rock fill for our driveway. When our others subsequently kidded, my mother was convinced that their dams, having learned their lesson, taught the young ones not to eat laurel. Whether this was true or not, the kids did in fact live to be sold off. The does would then be rebred, and a new round of kids would shortly appear.

My brother with cat and goat on our front path
(Wilton, Connecticut, 1952)

In the beginning, we had two sheds, one bigger than the other. Eventually all the goats were sold off, and we kept the smaller shed as a doghouse, a singular remnant of our failed farming experiment in the New England woods. The goats had been my mother's idea. With her teenage live-off-the-land naïveté, she imagined raising and selling both meat and milk, and my father, a sculptor and city boy, bought into the scheme. Who would buy goat meat, though? Italians? Hispanics in Bridgeport? My parents had no clear idea, nor did they have the heart to butcher goats themselves. Complicating their hope for earnings was the state regulation requiring milk's pasteurization. Eventually, the whole goat plan had to be abandoned. Did my father burn the larger shed? I would think I'd remember the odor, sifting ashes for charred hardware. I do recall a lightning strike and a neighbor's barn burning, illuminating the night sky for miles around.

I believe I have inherited some of my young parents' back-to-the-land idealism, perhaps because I was born in the midst of this endeavor. I would never portray our family as impoverished. My parents owned a little land: they may have been chronically broke, but my father bargained at the town market for discolored meat or purchased bulk frozen vegetables by the carton. We froze some of what we grew ourselves. An artist with a teenaged wife, my father embraced the challenge enthusiastically, believing that he could supplement our monthly budget by gathering seafood at the nearby coast or picking fruits and berries in the woods. He dammed part of our stream with fieldstones in the hope it would swell for pickerel, maybe bass. At the same time, he'd see sculptural forms in wood and discarded metal—found art. Even now, my father's theories for his own photography are based on notions of hunting and gathering, finding the compositional gem among the weeds of the ordinary. Still thrifty in his late eighties, he continues to buy expired food on discount.

Now in the later years of my life, I am recovering some of my parents' early spirit, or at least finding myself deeply curious about what can be gathered, caught, and harvested on my own property. My wife, Mary, and I have spent many years restoring an old country house in Burgundy that we bought on a whim before we were married. When my mother retired, she moved to Paris and soon after came to live with us. As a result of her efforts, we now have herb and vegetable gardens and chickens, and discuss acquiring goats so often that we refer to our "imaginary goats" as if this ghostly flock actually existed.

Over time I have learned that in temperate zones one can walk practically anywhere in nature and forage like a goat. A kind of twenty-first-century cult called "wildcrafting" has emerged out of deep nostalgia for a planet that once sustained wildernesses. I have often tried to put my finger on the driving force behind this movement. Is it the wish to recover traditional knowledge of foods in nature? Is it a fantasy of achieving self-reliance, or a belief in the purity of early native customs? Or are we distracting ourselves from inexorable disasters, personal and global, through a childlike focus upon natural things?

As a child growing up in the woods and spending summers on the nearby shore, I wasn't thinking that way. Becoming self-reliant and developing survival skills was simply fun. But for my father, born during the Depression, the idea of something-for-nothing had a moral significance. He abhorred waste in any form. To his mind, thrift, bargains, sales, bartering, and secondhand anything stood for the greater good. Our food-gathering forays verged on transcendence to a state of grace. And my mother, having spent parts of her childhood around professional chefs in New York City and on Nantucket, became a gifted cook in her own right. She treasured the freshest, most flavorful foods, and her enthusiasm motivated us just as much as something-for-nothing did. Collection, preparation, cooking, and dining were all woven together into the pleasures of the day. This exact sensation comes to me now when I return home with a bag full of mushrooms I've gathered, and we sit together cleaning off the leaf litter and soil, discussing whether we'll try a risotto, or quiche, or soup.

Returning to country life in Burgundy has led me to a new arena of discovery in cooking and natural foods while affording visceral associations with my childhood. The outgrowth of this eclectic experience is a sort of "commonplace book" that includes notes on correspondences of place and taste, memories, literature, art, science, and recipes. I hope you'll enjoy it.

IN PURSUIT OF WILD EDIBLES

1

WEBS OF HEAVEN AND EARTH

I COMB THE CONTOURS of the forest floor, the leaf rot, fallen trees, the vague paths as if I were looking for lost keys. My friend Jean-Pierre Campagne walks ten yards away, searching the ground with the same attentiveness but a far more educated eye. These are the woods of his country; I'm just a guest here, though a permanent one. Gunshots erupt, then the sounds of horns and men shouting in the distance. Hunting season begins in Rogny as thrillingly as a small war.

Despite our solemn appearance, however, Jean-Pierre and I are merely searching for mushrooms in the Bois de Dreux, a short back-road drive from Rogny-les-Sept-Écluses, the canal village in which my wife and I own an eighteenth-century presbytery. The old house is situated next to an eleventh-century church on a hill that was of strategic value to the invading Romans during the Gallic Wars.

Our village lies in a region of northwest Burgundy called La Puisaye, derived from a combination of Celtic words meaning "ponds" and "woods." Although it's only ninety miles from Paris, La Puisaye is a part of France that even the French don't know well, except for those who pass through on pleasure barges navigating the Briare Canal, the oldest artificial waterway in Europe. Built under the auspices of Henry IV, the canal links two of France's seven great *fleuves,* the Seine and Loire. Considering that this is a land of ponds and forests, it comes as no surprise that it is also a land of moss and mushrooms.

Though Jean-Pierre and I hunt for mushrooms in the same variegated light, rooting under the same canopy of oak, hornbeam, and birch trees, I can't help thinking we are looking at two different forests, two different worlds. Jean-Pierre grew up in Pau, the departmental capital of the

Pyrénées-Atlantiques, where his parents ran an *auberge,* a combination hotel-restaurant. Given its sizable population, Pau is a true *ville,* but it is also sited on the northern edge of the Pyrénées separating France from Spain, and thus retains some elements of the wild in two countries largely devoid of wilderness.

Jean-Pierre's childhood family life may not have been charmed, as I imagine mine to have been. He had a brooding, volatile father he feared and a fretting mother trapped in a working marriage. The two partnered in an enslaving business as chef and hostess respectively.

"I have a fond memory of my first time collecting mushrooms," Jean-Pierre tells me. "I went with my mother to hunt for *rosés des prés.* She was happy, I was happy, we felt free—something very rare for us." *Rosés des prés* are regarded as the best of the *champignons de Paris,* a variety one finds year-round in the markets.

For Jean-Pierre the forest became a refuge. He was sent for whole summers to a mountain *colonie de vacances,* a highly organized French version of children's summer camp. His Basque cousin, a survivalist type who caught trout barehanded under rocks in cold rivers and crayfish in sawmill river channels, served as a kind of trail master. He also taught Jean-Pierre to find cèpes. These large mushrooms are greatly prized for their meaty flesh, fruity earth odor, and nutty taste. They can be made into sumptuous soups and sauces, and are stellar in risotto and pasta recipes.

A misfit throughout his *lycée* years, Jean-Pierre—like many young people in the late 1960s—found no appeal in university studies. He chose instead the utopian life of a theater commune set up on a farm in the Ariège, a rugged part of the Pyrénées southeast of Pau. With this group of artists and idealists who romanticized "living off the land," he fell easily into country chores: milking goats, growing organic vegetables, and collecting wild edibles. *Girolles,* known in English as chanterelles, became a personal favorite because of their color (ranging from soft yellow to vibrant orange), peppery apricot fragrance and flavor, and sensuous lipped cap, the most feminine of mushrooms.

Later on, Jean-Pierre became a journalist for Agence France-Presse, specializing in the political landscape of sub-Saharan Africa. He also became, to my ongoing dismay, a frontline war correspondent, covering conflicts in the Balkans, Afghanistan, Iraq, Gaza, Somalia, Rwanda, Libya, and Mali. He is now so acculturated to African life and its human extremes that he experiences a vacuum when he returns to the Paris bureau to write dispatches.

Jean-Pierre reminds me of Ishmael, who confides in the opening pages of Melville's *Moby-Dick* that "whenever my hypos get such an upper hand of me, that it requires a strong moral principle to prevent me from deliberately stepping into the street, and methodically knocking people's hats off—then, I account it high time to get to sea as soon as I can." In Jean-Pierre's case, substitute "Africa" for "sea." When he stays with us in Rogny, he goes barefoot even in winter, and wraps boldly printed African mud cloth at his waist as a skirt. Often, a novel or short story set four thousand miles away is developing in his mind. It is clear that, at these times, he yearns to flee France. Here in the woods, though, he seems abstracted from all that.

Is hunting for mushrooms a metaphor for the pursuit of something more essential? Maybe. As Thoreau famously observed, "Many men go fishing all of their lives without knowing that it is not fish they are after." Mushroom hunting, too, is a way of hushing a mind full of chatter, of paying close attention to one's own senses, of noticing, and above all of recovering. A lovely idea, but something simpler also drives Jean-Pierre and me: we want to find mushrooms.

I grew up in the woods, and though I have spent most of my time since childhood living in cities and now work in Paris, the country remains a fundamental part of my psyche. My mother, a runaway, took up modeling in New York City before she was sixteen. Strong-willed, she made up her mind to marry an artist, start a family, and use the land productively. Deer may have decimated everything my parents planted, our goats may have poisoned themselves, and marauding foxes may have dashed off with our ducks, but our small and solitary forest world was powered by the rhythms of nature.

Behind our house, the East Branch Silvermine River rushed over rocks, pooled, and snaked half a mile through woods before passing the empty foundations of a mill and feeding into Browns Reservoir. It could have been a scene rendered by Cousins or Constable. Even at the earliest age, I knew that mine was a blessed childhood, one that my impetuous teenage

My mother and father just before moving to the woods (New York City, 1950)

mother created for us, one with no discernible gods—just trees and animals, stars and storms.

If my mother was the inventor of our life, my father helped fuel it by becoming a consummate hunter-gatherer. My brother and I joined him on his Saturday-morning forays, scavenging at the town dump for objects to furnish our house or transform into sculptures. We'd spearfish with him, or pry oysters from rocks in coves, or dig clams on the salt flats. We'd head off into the woods to gather berries, apples, and hickory nuts.

I pictured myself as a hunter-gatherer, too, modeled after the Paugussett Indians, whose name means "where the river widens," and whose settlement sites are distinguished by heaps of oyster shells. On the mile-long walk from our dirt road to and from the school bus stop, I'd pass the ever-changing marsh with its skunk cabbage and jack-in-the-pulpits, a stand of oaks that creaked in the autumn breezes, and Gregory's Pond, which—after a spring thaw—magically acquired a dense population of turtles, frogs, and water snakes. While mushrooms fascinated me with their sudden emergence after a warm autumn rain, it never occurred to me to collect them. Only later would I learn that edible species, some with medicinal and spiritual powers, abound in the New England woods.

One can love mushrooms for their names alone: dryad's saddle, shaggy mane, blewit, chicken of the woods, turkey tail, and artist's conk. Many found in New England are closely related to those treasured in France: morels, black trumpets, chanterelles, king bolete, and hedgehog mushrooms. In my ignorance I picked them just for the novelty of their form or color, or their fragile flesh. Like all country kids I'd stomp on a puffball for the explosion of spores, unaware that they were not just edible but delicious. As a Paugussett Indian, I surely would have starved.

Growing up in isolation made me pathologically shy, a defect that alarmed my teachers. While mute, I was still a careful listener in school and remember a teacher reading to us something Ralph Waldo Emerson wrote: "I become a transparent eyeball; I am nothing; I see all; the currents of the Universal Being circulate through me." The image was emblazoned in my brain. As absurd as it sounds, I believe I understood New England Transcendentalism on some visceral level, though of course without its moral dimensions or the rejection of politics and religion. I hardly knew what organized religion was, never having been exposed to it, but I felt a form of spirit that lived in hues of light and the nuances of the seasonal changes. Nature's spontaneous moods drew me out of myself.

My only religious training came from one of my mother's transitory whims. At one point she decided that my brother and I were going to be Quakers. "If you are a Quaker," she explained, "you don't have to pledge allegiance to the flag or even pray. There are no ministers. Pray or don't pray. It's entirely up to you." Unlike my mother, though, I realized how revolutionary it would be not to pledge allegiance to the flag in Eisenhower's America, where we practiced shielding ourselves from nuclear blasts by scrambling under our desks or into our lockers. Still, my mother would rattle off beautiful Quaker words: peace, unity, simplicity, equality, and integrity. Who wouldn't want to be a Quaker? In my mildly confused child's mind, I thought the Paugussett Indians would probably have made good ones.

Our very brief Quaker period began memorably, my mother driving my brother and me to an obscure grove of snowbound pines brightened by a blaze of post-storm sunlight. A simple white clapboard house stood with a sign in black lettering that said "Friendship Meeting House." It was the most peaceful spot, secluded from one world, open to another. Inside, the light poured through austere glass windows. No one spoke. This was the silent waiting for the spirit among the pines.

In the same vein, it's hard to resist Emerson's exuberant declaration on the moral influence of the Universal Spirit coming to us through nature, the likenesses in things. Emerson's eccentric protégé Thoreau, who championed conscience over civil law, seduces us with descriptions of an unfettered solitary life at Walden. More than a century earlier, even Jonathan Edwards of "Sinners in the Hands of an Angry God" fame meditated, as a mere seventeen-year-old, on the lowly spider and saw glimmerings of God's grace: "I know I have several times seen, in a very calm and serene day at that time of year, standing behind some opaque body that shall just hide the disk of the sun and keep off his dazzling rays from my eye, multitudes of little shining webs and glistening strings of a great length, and at such a height as that one would think they were tacked to the sky by one end, were it not that they were moving and floating."

Jean-Pierre, on the other hand, grew up a French Catholic, believing that the one God was in truth three divine beings. As an altar boy, he piously performed his duties during Mass. In his country, nothing seems immune from the saints and possible apparitions, and the irony of my living in a former religious building in a foreign country hasn't been lost on me. As with many Catholics of our generation, adolescence unraveled Jean-Pierre's doctrinal faith, opening the door to the occult predictions of Tarot cards and the wisdom of the I Ching. Above all, he communed with the spirits of trees, perhaps expressing the residual druidic influence within his Gallic heritage. It was the perfume of the forest that fanned his desire for mushrooms.

While I didn't collect mushrooms as a child, I did learn that one could purchase a mail-order mushroom kit, and I decided to cultivate some. When the kit arrived, I discovered, to my great dismay, that horse manure was required. I took the instructions too literally, collected manure from a field, and spent weeks hovering over a trough of manure that refused to yield my mushrooms. Considering the likely presence of pathogens, this may have been a lucky disappointment.

As a teenager, I found the mystical possibilities offered by hallucinogenic mushrooms irresistible: you could take a "trip" without going anywhere. I naïvely ate my first mushroom in the wild at fifteen with a hippie friend who picked a shaggy parasol and said, "Eat this—it'll make you high." The mere suggestion seemed to make me high, so I decided it worked. At the time, my shaman/priests were Timothy Leary and Carlos Castaneda, and I was working hard on my alien systems of perception with psilocybin, a hallucinogenic compound found in nearly two hundred species of mushrooms. The ritualistic use of psilocybin mushrooms to attain higher states of consciousness stems back to Mesolithic times and has been credited with inspiring parietal art in different parts of the world. Just recently, scientists have been extracting drugs from "magic mushrooms" to treat severe depression. Robin McKie in the *Guardian* reports, "The drug appears to stop patients dwelling on themselves and their own perceived inadequacies." This might run counter to what Leary was after, but it seems to fit nicely with Castaneda's objectives.

In the 1950s and 1960s, federally funded research delved into the benefits and dangers of psychedelics, but ultimately came to a halt as a result of poorly designed scientific experiments. Hallucinogens were designated controlled substances and their possession made illegal. Now, serious investigations have been resurrected to see how mushroom-derived psychedelics can help terminally ill patients achieve a state of a consciousness that can transcend the constraints of disease. Psychedelic therapy that reduces the ego in favor of the "waking dream" has even been tried on alcoholics.

It's not clear how long fungiculture has existed among humans, but we do know that it has enjoyed only limited success. In the case of the button mushroom, the French author and soil scientist Olivier de Serres in the 1600s thought to dig up white mushroom mycelia to plant in beds of composted manure. In the late nineteenth century, the Pasteur Institute developed pure culture spawn for pathogen-free mushrooms. The Americans perfected its white color, anticipating the public's preference for white food, the same spirit that produced Wonder Bread.

My culinary experience of mushrooms during childhood, as for most Americans, was limited to toppings on pizzas or in Campbell's Condensed Cream of Mushroom Soup. My formal introduction to wild mushrooms didn't occur until my first trip to Europe. In Geneva, friends served me *sauté de veau aux morilles,* a veal stew with morel mushrooms. Morels are phallic-looking mushrooms with a spongy honeycombed tip that appear in the spring in the Jura and other mountainous regions, although neighbors in our village say they can be found in our local woods. They have an exquisite smoky earth flavor. On that same trip but in Florence, I sampled for the first time *risotto ai funghi* with *porcinis* and *tagliolini al tartufo,* pasta with shaved white truffles. In Madrid, I had the classic mixed wild mushroom and garlic tapas: *setas al ajillo.*

From this eye-opening trip, I brought back sachets of dried mushrooms for gifts. My mother, inspired by hers, mixed morels with button mushrooms in a duxelles preparation. (Duxelles—finely minced, sautéed mushrooms—are the invention of the great seventeenth-century chef François-Pierre de La Varenne, who coincidentally came from Burgundy.) Many years after this initial gift, my mother layered duxelles in the special version of white lasagna that she made for our wedding feast.

On our woodland expedition, Jean-Pierre and I not only observe the spider's "little shining webs and glistening strings of a great length," but are obliged to wipe them from our faces while defending ourselves from the branch-lash of saplings, wild plum and rose thorns, and horseflies that in autumn redouble their annoying ardor. It really is, in Thoreau-speak, "the fish" that we are after. True hunter-gatherers, we are thrilled to discover the perfect *bolet comestible* (*cèpe de Bordeaux*) and the prized black rather than brown-capped *tête-de-nègre,* a racist-sounding name that might make Americans flinch. We dream of finding swaths of sweet-tooth mushrooms or *pieds-de-mouton*—"sheep's feet"—or freshly emerged *girolles.* Sensing the right moment to look for mushrooms requires keen attention to rainfall, temperature, and the progress of the seasons. Often it is too dry, too cold, or too late. Nevertheless, mystery remains in the process. Sometimes mushrooms magically appear when you least expect them. Conversely, they may fail to show even under the best conditions.

Jean-Pierre makes the first find: an elderly cèpe, rotting, to be frank, with yellowish green mousse under its cap. The presence of mousse instead of gills is a distinguishing feature of cèpes. To my amazement, Jean-Pierre saves even the spoiled mushrooms to whittle them down later into questionable morsels. He is a true hunter-gatherer.

I am always looking for a beautiful *bolet,* with a bulging stem and a rust-brown hemispheric hat under which there is a fresh white mousse. Part of the wonder in finding a perfect edible mushroom is that there is stiff competition for them, particularly cèpes. More often than a round dome, one discovers gaping craters made by enormous red slugs or caves hollowed in the stem by small gray ones. Escargots cover them in slime, but at least these snails are wild edibles themselves, savored by the Romans, often served with mushrooms. Black beetles burrow through the white flesh, maggots cluster and wiggle, and tiny worms turn the interiors of the healthiest-looking cèpes into lace. Mice leave little telltale tooth marks, as do hedgehogs and squirrels. Deer and badgers devour them whole.

Perhaps no animal, even humans, can compete in mushroom gourmandise with the wild boar, whose population has exploded in our area and whose depredations are omnipresent. Cèpes are better known in the Anglophone world by the Italian name *porcini,* meaning "piglets." Since Roman times, porcini have been considered the mushrooms that hogs eat, or more simply hog mushrooms. Different countries have their own names for cèpes based on the local perception of the fungus. Among my favorite names come the Spanish *rodellon,* meaning "small round boulder," and the Dutch *eekhoorntjesbrood,* for "squirrel's bread." *Cèpe* in French is derived from the Latin *cippus,* ultimately referring to the mushroom's fat trunk or stem.

Rotted cèpe in hand, Jean-Pierre becomes so preoccupied by the search that he disappears into the woods directly toward the gunfire. It's as if he doesn't hear it, or is led zombie-like into the action after spending so much time in war zones. Sometimes I just think he is crazy. We are not wearing bright-green or orange safety vests, and I only give restrained calls and low whistles to Jean-Pierre. We are doing our best to remain discreet since, on entering the Bois de Dreux, we passed signs saying *propriété privée, defence d'entrer.* The simple translation is "Keep Out!" There are other signs that have the same basic message, even threats: *attention: pieges* (traps) or simply *vipers,* our local poisonous snake. Jean-Pierre and I are not only trespassing but also poaching, since by law the landowners own the mushrooms. There's no denying it: I have matured into a petty criminal, though I console myself by thinking that if I don't eat these mushrooms, certainly the wild boars and slugs will. Not so long ago, the forests were associated with aristocratic domains, and if I were transported a few centuries back, the penalty for my poaching might include the loss of my hand. Think of what happened to poor Jean Valjean in *Les Misérables* just for stealing an apple!

Unlike the New England woods, French forests have been highly managed for centuries. Forest experts thin the woods regularly, and selective cutting and reforestation are practiced nationwide. The forests near Rogny once provided firewood, charcoal, and beams for Paris, as the logs could be floated down the Loing River to the Seine or, later, transported by barges. Many of the forests have alleys cut through them for easy access, and for equitation. The forests in the Pyrénées would certainly feel less managed.

I've lost Jean-Pierre, but I know enough to drift toward the hunters to find him. I see numerous *bolets,* the family to which cèpes belong. While most have little culinary interest, I admire their majestic domes. Other mushrooms have gorgeous colors, intricate forms, and odd characteristics. The bold-red *amanite tue-mouches* is the mushroom that appears in lovely children's books and fairy tales. When it's crushed in milk, it attracts and poisons flies, hence its common English name, "fly agaric." The delicate cupped-flesh *pezize orangée* is as bright as mercurochrome. The *clavaire dorée* takes its name from its golden-yellow color: it resembles a mass of roots branching into the air. *Marasme à odeur d'ail,* as its name suggests, smells of garlic and develops a bell-shaped cap above an improbably tall, thin stalk.

Once I discovered an enormous parasitic mushroom growing at the base of an oak and took pictures of it to send to my friend Roger Ramond, a forestry professor, for identification. Roger wrote back, "That's a *fistuline hépatique.* The name comes from beef liver. Look around the same spot. You should find cèpes." The name was perfect; the mushroom resembled a beef liver stuck to a tree. However, instead of finding cèpes nearby, I discovered colonies of fresh *pieds-de-mouton.* I brought the beef liver mushroom home as a curiosity, leaving it on the kitchen table before leaving for Paris.

On the phone, my mother said, "Thank you for the lovely mushroom you left for me. I had it with fettuccini."

Apparently, then, it wasn't poisonous.

By the time I catch up to Jean-Pierre, he has harvested an impressive pile of dubious-looking cèpes.

"We're a week too late," I say, and hc agrees. Nevertheless, his mission is to collect mushrooms, and he has no intention of returning with an empty basket. I ask him if he ever collects mushrooms in Africa.

"None that I don't know well. I've found chanterelle-like mushrooms in Rwanda and Madagascar. I've eaten different things in Africa—camel, crocodile, kudu, antelope, ostrich, and oryx."

I can't erase the image of Jean-Pierre feasting on zoo animals from my mind.

"And *sauterelles vertes* in Lubumbashi," he adds. Green grasshoppers.

On returning to the presbytery, Jean-Pierre showers, puts on his mud-cloth skirt, and sits at the patio table. He begins trimming—or, more accurately, strip-mining—his rotted cèpes onto photos of fires and car wrecks in our local newspaper, *L'Yonne républicaine.* He cuts through the foot to remove the lacework of worms, forfeits the green mousse under the cap, and then slices the cap, finding white mushroom flesh that, remarkably, is still firm. He goes to work on the next, losing himself in his fragrant chore.

2

ON FAIRY RINGS AND MUSHROOM ROULETTE, FURTHER MUSINGS

MY INTEREST IN HUNTING for mushrooms didn't develop until after Mary and I had restored our presbytery, and financial circumstances and health issues brought my mother to live with us full-time. My childhood world, including the furniture I'd grown up with in Connecticut, suddenly materialized in northwest Burgundy. Once installed, my mother planted a productive kitchen garden and began keeping large, soft-feathered Australorp chickens for their beauty and their eggs. The hens maintain a healthy wild-edible diet that includes garden-devouring orange and black slugs. The curé's neglected orchard was restored through careful pruning and the introduction of healthy young cherry, pear, apple, plum, and nut trees. The hedges are laced with blackberry brambles, and wild strawberries blossom along the stone staircase and walls of the upper terrace.

I began noticing in our orchard and along our country roads a great variety of mushrooms emerging from one day to the next, depending on the caprices of weather. When I collected five fresh cèpes at the edge of a copse, my mother and Mary, both passionate eaters, were elated, and to verify that these were indeed edible mushrooms I showed them to two sisters, Jo and Véronique, who live in a very modest house next to the presbytery with their adoptive mother. Their true parents, Belgian barge owners, became marooned in Rogny during World War II while trying to deliver a hull load of sugar. The Germans had bombed one of the village bridges blocking passage, and the couple was able to survive the war partly by selling the sugar they had been hauling. Years later, when their children, the two sisters, were still young, the barge owners were both killed in a car wreck. An association of local Belgian immigrants found a foster home for them next to the presbytery while it was still serving as a curé's home. The girls, never fitting in socially with their peers, grew up as *genii loci* of our local woods. When my mother arrived, an outsider herself, the sisters instantly befriended her, helping her with small chores and bringing her wild edibles from the fields and forest, lovely mushrooms above all.

One misty morning, Véronique, carrying a woven basket with two sharp knives, arrived at our kitchen window and rapped at the pane. "If you are interested, I will show you places to find mushrooms," she announced to Mary and me. This is aberrant behavior, since all mushroom gatherers fiercely guard their secret mushroom spots. Véronique is decidedly different. She simply assessed the weather conditions and made up her mind that it was time to teach her neophyte American neighbors how to find French mushrooms.

Véronique established strict rules: "Do not touch mushrooms with your bare hands." This struck me as paranoid. She wore gloves and made sure we did the same. "Respect each mushroom, she insisted. "Leave it undisturbed even if it is poisonous. All living things have a role to play in the dynamic of the forest." We might be trespassers and poachers, but at least, through Véronique's discipline, we were conscientious about the forest itself.

I discovered that cèpes were well camouflaged despite their size, and I spent a good hour zigzagging among trees and periodically bending down and brushing away leaves before I found one. Véronique already had gathered half a basketful, and Mary had discovered a special knack for differentiating patterns and forms, something that has served her well behind a microscope during her career as a biologist. Mary discovered a black cèpe, and Véronique pronounced her "blessed with a good eye." Véronique then carefully cut the mushroom at ground level and performed some of the preliminary cleaning on the spot. I started pondering the mysteries of how we humans see. Do forms become imprinted in our brains over time, or is it simply a matter of intuition? As Véronique and Mary steadily filled the basket, I began to worry that I might have some sort of mushroom-spotting dyslexia. Conceding this possibility, I decided that bad luck played its part too, but both could be overcome by pure determination.

It would be several years before Jean-Pierre and I would begin to look for mushrooms together each autumn. Having recourse to his expertise helped me hone my instincts, and with experience I became more intrepid about exploring new mushroom-rich territories. Even when we are not together, Jean-Pierre and I enthusiastically swap mushroom-hunting news, as well as tales of a more personal nature. His life, like mine, has taken some improbable turns. After a bout with cancer, he has become more invested in the lives of his son and daughter. Jean-Pierre is also obliged to spend more and more time in Pau in his childhood home looking after his Alzheimer's-stricken father, who stares at him and demands repeatedly, "Who are you?" His mother, suffering from heart failure, requires attention. After his brother-in-law died unexpectedly, his sister gave birth to child with a severe defect. Belatedly, these calamities have pulled him into the vortex of a domesticity he had spent his life artfully evading.

He still resists the bondage of mortgages and ownership, except for a small *grange* in the Pyrénées without running water or electricity. The *grange* is a simple shelter, not unlike Thoreau's, only a good deal larger. While there this summer, he wrote, "It's too dry this year in the mountains for mushrooms. I still found a few *girolles* today. Good to escape the hell my father is living." When he was young, he'd spend days in his *grange* enjoying simplicity and solitude; now he goes there to heal, or to recover.

My more-or-less formal education in gathering mushrooms continues in south central France. Mary learns of a Fête des Champignons in the very old mountains of the Massif Central and proposes we take a weekend in early October to learn in the field from mycologists as we collect specimens and attend talks and exhibitions. The local chefs perform outdoor demonstrations of the classic mushroom dishes: *velouté de champignons, risotto aux cèpes,* and *fricassée de champignons sauvages.* Unfortunately their stoves, set up in the town square, are as temperamental as the chefs themselves: burner failures trigger memorable public tantrums.

On a morning that mixes frost with bright, glittering sunlight, we join a largish group of cheerful mushroom gatherers, baskets on arms and knives at the ready. We are divided into subgroups, each assigned a mycologist. Ours is a thin, serene Asian man in his sixties, dressed more like a mystic than a scientist. As we deploy in the forest, he lectures to anyone willing to listen, so Mary and I follow him closely, learning additional important rules: Don't collect mushrooms in plastic bags because the humidity and lack of air causes rot and ensuing toxicity. Look for the "universal veil" or the "partial veil" to identify the deadly amanitas. Avoid picking mushrooms along heavily trafficked roads because mushrooms concentrate heavy metals, chemicals, and even radiation, evidence of which has turned up in the wild boars that eagerly devour nonpoisonous mushrooms. To the dismay of hunters, radiation levels in boar muscles are far above those acceptable for human consumption. Even today, mushrooms continue to concentrate fallout from the radioactive Chernobyl cloud that passed through a large swath of eastern and western Europe.

Mary and I learn to follow the tenets of mushroom-collecting etiquette. Paramount among these is selecting, whenever possible, mushrooms mature enough to have released spores, and cutting their stalks high enough to leave the underground mycelia undisturbed. Mushrooms are only the fruiting bodies of a subterranean fungal system that takes the form of long, branching, hair-like strands called mycelia. If unraveled from a single tablespoon of soil taken from nearly anyplace, the resident mycelia could extend for miles. Systems of these strands originate from a fine dusting of spores released by the gills under the cap of a mushroom. In the case of cèpes, the mousse under the cap is composed of myriad small spore-producing tubes. Mycelia develop from spores and spread. When they merge with another set of compatible filaments, a new fruiting body emerges, given the humid seasonal conditions required for rapid swelling and growth.

The further one delves into the world of fungi, the more astonishing the discoveries become. Some derive carbon nutrients from dead vegetal or animal material as they contribute to the decomposition of wood and leaves, producing rich humus. Entire dead trees can be cleared away from the forest floor by microscopic mycelia. Other fungi are parasitic, living off weakened yet living plants and animals. But many live symbiotically. Mycelia provide essential minerals to tree root hairs; trees, in turn, supply vital carbon compounds to the mycelia. Mushrooms tend to hook up with preferred trees: truffles, for example, love dying oaks. Cèpes, chanterelles, and *pieds-de-mouton* may be found under oaks, too, but these are less fussy and also appear under conifers and hornbeam. Fungi help orchids germinate and flower. Algae unite with symbionts to create lichen. Both ambrosia beetles and certain ants cultivate fungi as a food source, and wood wasps lay their eggs among nutritious spores of a wood-rooting fungus. Yeasts and molds have brought us alcohol, soy sauce, penicillin, LSD, and Roquefort cheese; misery has been caused by rice blast, potato blight, yeast infections, cave disease, ringworm, and oral thrush. Many of these beneficial and detrimental fungi belong to a class known as Deuteromycota—"second fungi"—and reproduce asexually. Perhaps the greatest benefit of fungi lies in the mycelia that bind all soils together, holding and stabilizing up to thirty thousand times their own mass.

Our talkative mycologist adviser informs us that there are scientists and farmers who believe in a myco-utopia (often fused as mycotopia), achieving a balanced environment through innovative use of mycelia's healing powers. Some contend that mycelia can be engaged in "mycorestoration" through which oil spills can be metabolized, radiation contamination absorbed, and new medicines produced. Paul Stamens, mycologist and author of *Mycelium Running: How Mushrooms Can Save the World,* writes: "I believe that mycelium is the neurological network of nature. Interlacing mosaics of mycelium infuse habitats with information-sharing membranes. These membranes are aware, react to change, and collectively have the long-term health of the host environment in mind." I can't help thinking that Stamens may be one-upping Leary and Castaneda, suggesting that we share consciousness with the very vehicle, mushrooms (psilocybin, of course), that can liberate us from the ego to merge with a collective awareness of all living things.

While in the hills contemplating such metaphysics, Mary and I find several perfect cèpes that had not been attacked by predators, and, ill-equipped to cook them, we simply stop at a market, buy olive oil and salt, and sit on a hilltop graced with a Christian shrine. We picnic on delicious raw mushrooms while sipping Châteauneuf-du-Pape from the Rhône Valley.

Jean-Pierre and I frequently exchange digital photographs of the edible riches we find in the forest. I send him photos from our apprenticeship weekend and, soon after, more images of a large bowlful of cream-colored *pieds-de-mouton,* or hedgehog mushrooms. These had been meticulously cleaned of the spore needles that are often compared to a cat's raspy tongue or the spines of a hedgehog, the source for its name in English. Jean-Pierre's return image is a pile of cèpes—some with suspect form and varying stages of rot—that he collected with his grandson Mathieu on a bonding vacation near us on the Loire. The next picture is of a delicious-looking *poêlée de champignons persillés.* Jean-Pierre writes, "Mathieu and I would like to stop by the Presbytery. Okay?" I wonder if I am ready to eat mushrooms a six-year-old has collected.

Stories of poisonings are ubiquitous. During his residency, a doctor friend of mine interrogated one writhing patient.

"It's the *champignons* I ate. I know it."

"What kind?"

"Trumpets of death."

"But they are edible."

"*Trompettes de la mort,* I tell you!"

Even my own doctor, an ardent lover of nature and natural foods, refuses to collect wild mushrooms, though he knows that all French pharmacists are highly trained in identifying toxic species. You need only walk to a pharmacy with a basket of mushrooms to receive a verdict. Nevertheless, I admit to feeling queasy when dining with French friends who, while glowing from an afternoon of *apéritifs,* serve wild mushrooms that "Grandmother found this morning!" or that the town drunk left on the windowsill as a generous neighborly gift. It's a French version of Russian roulette. To make the danger all the more real, the entire village knows and is not reluctant to recount from thirty years ago that our closest neighbor accidentally (and memorably) served her family amanitas. The meal killed her husband and two of her four children.

Ninety-five percent of mushroom-related deaths are attributed to amanitas. From that genus, the death cap (*Amanita phalloides*) alone is responsible for 50 percent, and the destroying angel (*Amanita virosa*) comes in a close second. Both the death cap and the destroying angel are white and, when emerging, can be confused with both common button mushrooms and puffballs. It is strongly advisable to cut fresh puffballs in half in order to verify their structure. The surest sign of an amanita is remnants of the egg-shaped sac called the volva, from which the mushroom emerges. The remnants appear at the base of the stem and on the stem itself. Unfortunately, death caps and destroying angels have a pleasing flavor, and symptoms are delayed for hours, if not days, making diagnosis difficult. Amanitin toxins inhibit the enzyme responsible for the synthesis of RNA from DNA, rapidly halting cell metabolism and causing failure of vital organs. Mushrooms in the amanita family are among the most common in the Bois de Dreux, and some are legitimate wild edibles.

Mushrooms can cause varying degrees of illness. Delicious wild mushrooms, more than most wild edibles, induce frenzied something-for-nothing greed, at times clouding good judgment. Italo Calvino begins one of his classic collections with a story about Marcovaldo, a modest working family man, coveting wild mushrooms that he finds in the city, ready to swell with one night's rain. To his chagrin, he also discovers that a street sweeper was eyeing the same prize. When they both go to collect mushrooms, Marcovaldo's anger toward the street sweeper turns to generosity, and he invites bystanders to collect mushrooms too. All end up in the hospital:

> They all found plenty of mushrooms, and lacking baskets used their open umbrellas. Somebody said: "It would be nice to have a big feast, all of us together!" But, instead, each took his own share and went home.
>
> They saw each other again soon, however, that very evening, in fact, in the same ward of the hospital, after the stomach pump had saved them all from poisoning. It was not serious, because the number of mushrooms eaten by each person was quite small.
>
> Marcovaldo and Amadigi [the street sweeper] had adjacent beds; they glared at each other.

Mushrooms are inherently intriguing. The range of colors, shapes, and odors make them alluring. Walking back to the car after gathering mushrooms one afternoon, I spotted a curious arc of large, ivory-colored specimens with broad funnel caps. On closer inspection, I saw that the arc was in fact an enormous ring running through a marsh, the fruiting bodies standing about eight inches off the ground. I've seen mushroom rings before, but nothing like this, nothing so stunning. Small mushroom rings conjure up images of Celtic fairies dancing in the mist while sage-looking toads poised on amanitas gaze on. The French call such formations *ronds de sorciers*—sorcerers' circles. (A German would call it a witches' ring, a *Hexenring*.) The phenomenon occurs when the central and oldest mycelia grow too dense and die off, while vigorously producing at the periphery of the necrotic zone.

It's easy to see how a fairy ring of such immensity would engender superstition. La Puisaye has, in common with New England, a legacy of superstition, inspiring legends of vampires, werewolves, and *les dames blanches.* Anyone who dances with fairies and witches is of course likely to come to a bad end. Cotton Mather, the Puritan minister, was convinced that witches and devils loitered about in the forest, looking for opportunities to steal souls. In *Wonders of the Invisible World,* justifying his prosecution of witches, Mather wrote, "In all the Witchcraft which now Grievously Vexes us, I know not whether any thing be more Unaccountable, than the Trick which the Witches have, to render themselves and their Tools Invisible." One wonders what a meeting of this visionary son of Increase Mather, Harvard's first president, and Timothy Leary, Harvard's guru of LSD and mastermind of the Psilocybin Project, would be like.

On returning to the presbytery, I sit at the kitchen table with an eight-inch-long fairy-ring mushroom and a mushroom identification guidebook, my mother and Mary mildly interested.

"I found it," I announce. "Edible when young."

Neither woman wants to try it. I point to an impressive name: *Infundibulicybe geotropa,* also known as trooping funnel or monk's head. The world's largest fairy ring exists in France, we learn: formed from *Infundibulicybe geotropa,* it's nearly a half mile in diameter and approximately seven hundred years old.

Mary says, "I still won't eat it."

By October in France, one feels the aperture of daylight closing ever earlier. The *Infundibulicybe geotropa* is relegated to ornament status, while my mother makes a *tarte aux cèpes* with prosciutto and both shallots and garlic. Over a bottle of Santenay, we argue the merits of cooking cèpes with shallots versus garlic: proponents of nouvelle cuisine shun both additions, while traditionalists call for one or the other.

The next weekend, with a light rain falling, Mary and I drive past a fallow field where we spot what looks like three large globes made of limestone. Baffled, I halt the car and reverse to get a better look. Standing in the field, we gawk at the globes that come up almost to our knees. Stretching out a hand, I feel the familiar soft surface and firm meat of a mushroom. I have our dog Jake pose next to the globes so I can take photographs that give an accurate sense of height and volume. The two globes dwarf the little dog. Back at the presbytery, Mary and I thumb through the mushroom guide to *vesse-de-loup géante,* a giant puffball. In French, *vesse-de-loup* means wolf's flatulence. Leave it to the French to come up with an indelible metaphor. Like the *Infundibulicybe geotropa,* the *vesse-de-loup géante* is edible when young, and the guidebook asks us to imagine feeding an extensive family on one mushroom. It also advises caution: the early growth can easily be confused with a death cap. My mind, though, is far from poisonous things. Drifting, I imagine a boy taking a leap, stomping with both feet, and disappearing into a cloud of spores.

3

ARIEL'S GHOST

MY DOCTOR SAYS I need to learn how to Zen-out more, so to calm myself I've taken to calling up a mental cinema of bucolic scenes from my New England childhood. Many images are of the seaside. In one, I'm standing on a point between Compo Cove and Sherwood Millpond in Westport, Connecticut, squinting at the far shore in search of the distant figure of my father. I'm seven, maybe? He's using a screwdriver to pry off oysters crusted on rocks or digs for large clams in the clay shallows. I often lose him altogether when the shadows settle in below the reeds, but he always reemerges. Swimming to the edge of the cove, he lifts his diving mask to his forehead, clears his sinuses, and hands me a drawstring net sack laden with mollusks he's harvested at the delicate convergence of creek water and tidal sea marsh. I would learn later that the biological alchemy of salt and sweet water makes the area a rich breeding zone for diverse sea creatures, and in turn a life source for the Native American tribe I romanticized as a child.

The name "Compo" comes from the Paugussett word *compaug*, meaning "bear's fishing ground." The spot was also once called Machamux, "beautiful land." I wonder how many native variations of the same word existed up the Eastern Seaboard of North America.

In my memory, these evenings gathering seafood with my father came about a decade before serious dead zones began to form in Long Island Sound, especially in its western end, from industrial pollution, toxic runoff, and sewage. Dad's shoreline foraging evolved in stages, starting with his purchase of a mask and snorkel. The mask was a bit abnormal, made up of three glass panels. "It always leaks," he would complain. I don't know where he found it. Later, he fashioned a pole spear out of a wooden rake handle and a three-pronged point fastened with a nail—a makeshift trident. It might have been great for gigging flounder at night, the way it's done from the Carolina shores to the Gulf of Mexico, but Dad's trident was the source of many frustrated narratives: large fish swimming past and vanishing, barely grazed; eels writhing off the barbs in the most horrifying way.

In order to increase the amount of time he was able to spend in the water, he mail-ordered a do-it-yourself diving-suit kit, and in our living room cut out and pieced together neoprene with black glue, like a tailor from the old neighborhood. The glue's toluene promptly rendered the whole family light-headed, especially my father, alcohol-intolerant and the cheapest drunk I know.

Summer evenings, when Dad got off work, my brother and I would pile into the car with him when there was still plenty of light. Sometimes my mother came along, and we would cook out in the Sherwood Island Park at twilight. Once it got too dark for him to see, my father would come back to join us. In the summer we were never indoors for very long.

Recently, I visited Dad, now eighty-eight, in a subsidized housing complex that is home to many Russian immigrants, maybe ten miles from Compo. He's converted his modest efficiency into a photography studio, and instead of keeping food fresh in his refrigerator, he packs it with chemicals and photographic paper with varying degrees of light sensitivities for contrast, materials difficult to find now. I tell him about the sentimental childhood images I run and rerun in my head to lower my blood pressure. "It works," I insist. "It's like TM, but they call it 'restful awareness.'"

Thinking back, Dad muses, "There used to be a restaurant on the cove that had hard rubber mats under water. They let clams and oysters clean themselves in the cove."

Could he be talking about Allen's Clam and Lobster House? I decide against pursuing the topic.

"Yeah, it was fun taking a pailful of those oysters home occasionally," he adds. My therapeutic images dissolve suddenly into crime-scene photos of my father's stealthy clam and oyster raids, with me his unwitting accomplice. Maybe I just have a suspicious mind. Nevertheless, I've always taken a little pride in his scofflaw ways.

I was never entirely sure what he was up to in those days, but I know he believed that by foraging we'd save money on food and, more importantly, have a good time. When you're born into a certain way of life, you think everyone is living the same way. Or maybe you know better, and you still like the fact that your family is just a little different. What my father may have lacked as a farmer he more than made up for as a hunter-gatherer. Not just for wild edibles, either, but for almost anything useful, ornamental, or curious, including Paugussett relics. Even now, in old age, he finds them. Periodically, he'll present his "evidence" to the office of the Connecticut state archaeologist and receive a boilerplate letter in return: "Your information has been noted."

My collection of shoreline images increased significantly as our foraging territory began to expand up the coastline to Rhode Island's South Shore. In those days, a twenty-five-cent toll plaza came up about every ten miles on I-95, and my father knew how to circumvent each one. He purchased an old station wagon, a one-quart-of-oil-per-hundred-miles smogmaker one breakdown away from the junkyard, for one hundred dollars and equipped it with oversized tires, which he referred to as "baldinos." These were glassy-smooth, worn free of tread, and, of course, illegal. Because tires had tubes in them back then, he was able to let the air out of them for greater traction. We would arrive at night to avoid detection and drive dune buggy–style over beaches and sandy spits. Since maintaining forward momentum was critical, the system wasn't perfect.

We generally camped tentless on the dunes, so by morning our heavily dew-soaked sleeping bags felt like cold mashed potatoes. At sunrise, Dad would shake talcum powder into his suit so that the sleeves and pants slipped over his skin easily, and then wade in between knotted wrackweed and kelp. He was often successful in spearing blackfish and striped bass among the mussel-encrusted rocks, and flounder in sandy channels with strong tidal currents. He had a relatively advanced spear gun, the tips of which he sharpened on rocks or with a file. Conveniently, the point screwed off so that fish could be slipped easily off the skewer.

My brother and I had our own snorkeling equipment and learned to spot the telltale eyes of flounder above the sandy bottom where they'd bury themselves. We'd poke around the bivalve holes underwater in the sand for quahogs, steamers, and razor clams, or strip mussels from the rocks, or pick up bay scallops off the bottom of a cove. Startled blue

My father, Joseph Greene, in 1962
(New Haven, Connecticut)

crabs flashed their sapphire line claws at us and then swiftly scooted off sideways.

As a kid, it never occurred to me that using diving equipment for seashore foraging might be prohibited, or that I needed a license. Random clam raking and use of shovels leaves craters and disturbs everything, whereas diving feels like going to nature's seaside market and selecting the choicest produce with a minimum of environmental disturbance. What we didn't eat raw we wrapped in foil, the crinkled silver packets blackening on driftwood coals in a ring of surf-polished rocks.

My father was a gleaner in the shoreline potato fields as well, considering the small discarded spuds to be as good, if not better, than "officially" harvested ones. The only things we paid for were corn and tomatoes bought from roadside stands. Our meals couldn't have been simpler or fresher, the only ancillary ingredients being butter, salt, and pepper, maybe lemon. While as a kid I didn't have the current knowledge of the benefits of Omega-3s and vitamin D from fish on brain health and moods, I always knew that fish consumption produced a sense of well-being.

During the picnics of my childhood, the rangers never bothered us about our beach fires or trespassing: indeed, part of the area was set aside for the legal recreation of surfcasters and four-wheel-drive campers. All together, rangers and campers and fishermen, we made a savvy, self-reliant tribe, or so I imagined. The night surfcasters used eels for bait, wading out toward the wave break and launching their hook rigs into the black air. They'd let out line as they brought their rods back up the beach to plant them in the sand. Even then, night fishing epitomized restful awareness for me: not much talk, just a cigarette glow or a neighbor's fire glimmering in the dark.

When my family moved from our Wilton house to New Haven, I had a primal sensation of fracture: almost nothing would be the same. What never changed, though, was my enthusiasm for diving. On my tenth birthday, my parents bought me a real U.S. Divers neoprene suit with a nylon lining, yellow trim, and aqualung insignia—a transformative gift. Within a year, my father and I had scuba tanks, and by age eleven I'd been awarded an underwater diver's certificate (necessary to refill tanks) after passing a decompression test far beyond New Haven Harbor one stormy Saturday morning, in water so dark at sixty feet that only the knots in the rope and the dull glint of my examiner's mask oriented me. I remember feeling a clamshell in the suspension of silt and seawater that was the ocean floor. Bringing it up, I beheld a token from the dark middle of nowhere, the closest experience I'd ever have to landing on the moon.

Soon after, Dad began to discover numerous lobster pots in Woodmont, just west of New Haven. Sealing some plastic flashlight torches with silicone, he would take us out on evenings with a bright moon and low tide to dive for lobsters. Shale formations jutted out from shore, so we armored ourselves well with suits, torches, and heavy gloves for protection against sharp rocks and powerful claws. Memories of night dives still inflect my dreams; images of phosphorescence and slowed sea life simultaneously attracted and blinded by the beam. I'm fortunate, I suppose: I have both

Me at age ten in 1962
(Rocky Neck State Park, Connecticut)

flying dreams and breathing-cool-air-underwater dreams, and neither type is ever bad. No doubt our probing underwater lights attracted plenty of attention from passing strollers and lovers seeking privacy in the rock cove. Was my father after the lobster pots themselves? Probably. But we caught lobsters at night; I know that much.

I'm not sure where Dad's love for the ocean comes from. He was a New York City kid who grew up eating hot dogs and swimming at Coney Island, but he's always understood the sea in ways that I still don't. He's been far braver, too, diving well into his eighties. After being sent to North Carolina State at the tender age of sixteen to learn textile design for the family business, he transferred to Tyler in Philadelphia, where his passion for art corrupted him—at least in the eyes of his parents, aunts, and uncles. But he ended up at King's Point Merchant Marine Academy and became an officer toward the end of World War II, transporting wheat to the leveled cities of Rotterdam, La Havre, and Odessa. He was in Manila when the war ended, and transported Jews who escaped eastward from Singapore to a new life in South America. And he steered seven-hundred-foot-long ships through Hell Gate, the Panama Canal, and other tight spots, not without some heart-stopping adventures.

Later, as a family man, he commanded our eight-foot, plywood sailing dinghy. Perhaps not the stuff of Conrad, but still invigorating. Plenty of excitement was available in the form of high winds, tidal currents, and the boat's own insistence on capsizing with the least provocation. The dinghy gave us access to rich seafood-gathering spots in salt ponds and bays that otherwise we wouldn't have been able to reach. Cautious and law-abiding people often advised us not to eat shellfish from Long Island Sound. Our activities accordingly shifted first to Newport and then Cape Cod, where after a long day's work our evening's entertainment might be the Provincetown Theater showing Dylan's *Dont Look Back*. "The vandals took the handles" would be playing in my head for days.

I'm remembering the night my brother and I took the boat out on Long Island Sound late into the night to fish. The Coast Guard was alerted, and our parents panicked. As we strayed down the coastline, we could see fish break the surface as if trying to taste the moon. It reminds me now of how the Chesapeake Indians used torches on their canoes to attract first plankton and then larger fish, or the fishing boats in the Algarve use strong lamps at night to draw squid and sardines to be netted. Or how I stood with my mother at the lit fishing docks in Galilee, Rhode Island, watching dozens of eels ribbon up to consume small fish at the surface.

Until my doctor told me, "Find ways to cool out," it hadn't occurred to me that feeling peaceful should be a goal of mine, nor did I think that foraging would be a calming activity. However, even at an early age I understood that memory is crafted. Picasso's 1939 painting *Night Fishing at Antibes* captures figures, fish, moon, stars, and gas lamps, all with the coming of the world's darkest years. Picasso's painting is all about fracturing.

Since acquiring a home in La Puisaye, land of rivers and ponds, and from my days at the shore dreaming about estuaries and gulfs in Brittany, Sardinia, Liguria, and elsewhere, I get the itch to purchase a small boat, something like the one my father bought, but preferably a highly portable and adaptable one. My aim is to reach less accessible areas, particularly in Europe, where there is no such thing as a place left untouched. My old instincts for gathering food at the sea are reviving as well. The fact is, though, that I have no place to keep a boat and can't really afford one.

All my naturalist friends urge me to consider a kayak, but I picture a boat that I could enjoy with Mary and friends like Jean-Pierre, and yet still operate alone when the occasion should call. I delude myself that even our dogs might serve as intrepid sailing mates. Since tidal currents shift in estuaries, I consider the advantages of a motor mount, but then a motor mount needs a motor too, an electric one I decide, adding a battery to the list. My birthday is in May, and Mary wants me to buy a boat for myself so that we can enjoy it over the summer.

Ultimately I decide on a canoe, even though I have little experience with one. There is something nearly perfect about them, a union of beauty and utility in their design. Canoes are often associated with Native Americans, but they have a considerable history throughout the world going back to Neolithic times. They were one of the key instruments of survival, not to mention of transport, exploration, and trade.

Leave it to the Canadians, with a long tradition in canoe building and use (including the birch-bark versions I thought as a kid represented the apex of water travel), to come up with a clever design for an inflatable one. The canoe I ultimately purchased resembles a very thin Zodiac with a motor mount: sleek, stable, and fast. It's twelve feet long but folds up to fit into the trunk of a small car. One person can easily handle it. Company ads show elegant, bikini-clad women paddling the canoe as if modeling it for a boat show in Cannes or Saint-Tropez. One can purchase an array of attachments, including swivel chairs and even a keel and a sail.

The inflatable canoe suits us perfectly, outside of the inevitable complications: delayed shipping dates and ultimately the question of how to get a Canadian canoe to Paris from European distributors in Holland, Germany, or Italy. Since shipping the canoe to Paris costs hundreds of euros, I choose to drive to Amsterdam, get a lesson in a warehouse on how to operate it, and then visit the Rijks and Van Gogh museums for a day. I'm tempted to make a maiden voyage through the city's canals, which shimmer with the reflections of centuries-old brick façades and bridges.

In the western suburbs of Amsterdam, the owner of the Dutch inflatable boat company meets me. He is not just typically tall, but impressively big and friendly. In perfect English (he speaks six languages), he tells me he gets the canoes from eastern Europe and North America, and goes to the Ukraine three times a year to oversee production of another line of boats he sells. Amid looming watercraft, he unfolds the little 12-foot Argus Discovery, explains the valve system, and with a foot pump blows it up in minutes.

The suburb is a marina town. Amsterdam is situated by the North Sea and Lake Markermeer, formerly open to the sea. It isn't lost on me that my boat would be perfect for this area. My friend Gereons Keuken Thuis wrote to me about the nearby wild edibles, coming up with a tagliatelle recipe just for me, one incorporating Dutch sea marsh foods including saltwort, sea lavender, and wild clams. Gereons knows my mother is half-Dutch: her maiden name, Van Blaricom, derives from Blaricum, a lovely town east of Amsterdam.

When I return to France, Mary marvels at our new canoe, easily inflating it herself after I demonstrate the foot pump and the ingenious valve system for its five air chambers.

"This canoe needs a name," I say. "Shelley's boat was called *Ariel,* or was it *Don Juan*? I know he and Byron argued about it. Each wanted to name it after a poem of his own, of course. What do you think about *Ariel's Ghost*?"

The canoe's light-gray hue reminds me of a ghost, and the ill-fated *Ariel* sank with Shelley and a crew of two.

"That's not funny," Mary replies, easily annoyed by morbid thoughts. (I still love the name.)

"John Steinbeck named his camper Roscinante in *Travels with Charley.* That seemed fitting for his wanderings."

"That's nice, but it's just a blowup boat," Mary points out. "It's not like you'll sail the seven seas in it."

With the name still pending, our maiden voyage takes place on Lac Bourdon, a reservoir near Saint-Fargeau famous for its tenth-century chateau, a former home of knights. Much later, it was the place of exile for Anne Marie Louise d'Orléans, known as "La Grande Mademoiselle" for her role in the seventeenth-century civil wars called the Fronde. Like most lakes near us, Lac Bourdon is murky but clean enough for swimming,

Mary and Jude with *Ariel's Ghost* (Lac du Bouchet, Auvergne)

and provides a protected environment for a spectacular array of birds, including heron, gulls, terns, cormorants, water hens, swallows, kingfishers, egrets, ducks, swans, osprey, and many others. Watercress grows in runoff gullies that feed the lake, and shells from freshwater clams litter the pebbly shore.

Lac Bourdon is a popular spot with anglers. Fishermen will pitch tents and set up racks of rods, mainly to catch *gardon, ablette,* pike, perch, perch-pike, eels, bream, and enormous carp. Once in a while someone will haul in a monstrous *silure,* an eastern European fish that now populates many of the lakes and larger rivers in France. It resembles a Mekong catfish and can easily be the size of whoever catches it, or larger. The local newspapers never miss an opportunity to feature a giddy fisherman hugging a gasping and bewhiskered *silure.* In appearance it is unmistakably your childhood nightmare come true, that unseen creature lurking underneath you when you're swimming; but finally it is just a big ugly fish that cleans lake and river bottoms. Everyone should feel privileged to swim with it.

The new canoe is so smooth-going and fast that it seems to fly on water. Mary and I take it on the Loire, the Yonne, the Cure. We paddle past thick woods and pastures, under low-hanging branches, through fast and slow stretches of water, spotting all manner of wildlife along the banks. We maneuver under bridges and by millraces. In rapids, the canoe dances, being so light. The two stabilizers in back help some, but we spin around in certain river currents, and the dogs are not thrilled by the experience.

For one day, the boat is christened *May Butterfly* after Rimbaud's "Drunken Boat" because it behaves a bit like a butterfly on water, and Rimbaud's poem is one of the first that deeply affected me when I was on the cusp of adolescence and social change seemed on track to become revolutionary:

> If I want a water of Europe, it is the black
> Cold puddle where in the sweet-smelling twilight
> A squatting child full of sadness releases
> A boat as fragile as a May butterfly.

When autumn rolls around, we drive down to the Landes and the Bay of Arcachon, an unusual basin opening to the sea, interrupting nearly 150 miles of sandy coast from the Geronde to Bayonne. At low tide the bay is nearly dry, leaving vast, muddy flats populated with egrets, storks, cormorants, gulls, and determined clammers. Prized crunchy saltwort stubbles the marshes with green succulent shoots. The largest sand dune in Europe, Dune du Pilat, was formed on the southwestern shore and looms strangely near the town of Arcachon. This resort community, created by the expansion of rail travel, is known for its architecturally unique Victorian villas. The area is also famous for oyster production, escapees cementing themselves to rocks and pilings.

Because the bay is a circumscribed natural feature, it is rare, delicate, and precious. River waters create some of the same fecundity that exists in Westport and Compo, and undoubtedly Neanderthals and later *Homo sapiens* benefited. Unhappily, an ill-chosen material used to paint the bottoms of boats poisoned the basin. It suffered first oyster gill disease and then a major oil spill, the after-effects of which you can still see.

We arrive at a launch, Mary inflates the canoe, and I secure the motor and connect the battery. In minutes, I'm pushing us offshore, the dogs clinging to us with their nails. Small ripples slap the bow, but the boat skims smoothly into the bay toward stark, encrusted pilings. We have never done this before, simply tie the boat up and chisel clustered oysters off a piling with a screwdriver. I rinse our bounty in a blue bucket of bay water and begin opening them, handing the first to Mary, no lemon, straight oysters. We picnic on oysters mid-bay in the early-autumn glare. Even our sea-wary dogs relax enough to try them.

4

THE WILDEST WILD OYSTER

LIKE MY FATHER, I became obsessed not only with gathering seafood but also with the forms and behavior of the creatures themselves, thriving as they were among huge mops of wrackweed or in the complex ecosystems of lagoons and saltwater ponds. Later in life, I learned that the French have a special expression for the sort of shoreline seafood gathering we did—*pêche à pied,* literally "fishing on foot." This doesn't mean simply feeling around in muck with one's feet for the edge of a quahog, as New Englanders might imagine. It involves a far broader spectrum of activities: gathering creatures that are stuck to rocks (mussels, barnacles, and oysters) or ones moving over rocks (periwinkles, limpets, and abalone); fishing by probing under rocks or in tide pools (mostly crabs); net-fishing between rocks or in brackish tidal marshes (eels and various types of shrimp); and digging in the sand (clams of all sorts).

Proper fishing on foot requires suitable tools. Standard equipment includes rake, clawed hand fork, a digging fork, a crab hook, various nets, a basket or pail, and rubber boots. While the French enjoy looking the part when it comes to skiing and cycling, two key national sports, one sees folks of all shapes, sizes, and ages with trowel in hand and plastic sacks. I've never seen a seaside forager with a ruler to follow size regulations. Foragers are enjoined to stay nearly a hundred feet away from oyster and mussel farming parks, which of course prove an attractive menace for those with my father's stealthy tendencies.

Even before I came to France, I had imagined *pêche à pied,* first from William Carlos Williams's playfully suggestive sea-snail poem "The Gentle Rejoinder."

These are the days that I want to
give up my job and join
the old men I once saw
on the wharf at Villefranche
fishing for sea-snails,
with a split stick

I can even hear Williams's raw American intonation as he pauses on words, as if to savor the very "thingyness" of them in his mouth, the audience laughing at the innuendo of the rejoinder.

I know
something else you could catch
she said, in the spring
as easily

This poem comes to mind when I see men, women, and children out with shovels and pails at low tide on the French shores, or netting shrimp in pools, or when I'd admire broad plein-air seascape paintings of Deauville, for example—locals with baskets collecting fruits of the sea via *pêche à pied.* And what of the many impressionist still-life paintings featuring seafood and wine, refreshingly sensuous in themselves, capturing the purity of composition, planes of light, and texture?

One of the most interesting factors in *pêche à pied* is that France has two coasts, and the North Atlantic one features dramatic tidal changes, especially during the phenomenon known as the *grandes marées* in the autumn and spring. Then a vast littoral zone is exposed, the area between the two tidal extremes. Because the tidal changes are enormous, *pêche à pied* can produce some surprises.

Mary's friend Pierre Legrain recounts, "Since we were little kids, my brother and I would gather *fruits de mer* near Carnac. Once we found a conger eel under a rock. *Incroyable!* Five feet long." Conger eels, considered delectable in France, can grow as large as eight feet or more and are reputed to be aggressive at times. It was not just the wonder of the exceptional find that lit up Pierre's face but the obvious nostalgia that *pêche à pied* evokes for the French.

Among the many revelations my move to France entailed was that a seafood feast, when based on crustaceans and mollusks, equaled a fête, or a party, particularly at Christmas and New Year's. One has to wonder if convincing evidence about the mood-boosting powers of Omega-3s could be gathered during these seafood-consuming binges. In their displays of oysters, clams, urchins, *tourteux,* spider crabs, *etrilles,* periwinkles, whelks, shrimp, langoustine, and even Breton or spiny lobsters, the restaurants, brasseries, and bistros of France seem to be welcoming customers to an Omega-3 fatty-acid high. The enticing creatures, along with pots of mayonnaise and the vinegar-pepper-shallot concoction called *mignonette,* are heaped on seaweed-covered ice to form a *plateau de fruits de mer,* which can be the monumental centerpiece of a table, rising three layers and feeding up to eight. Eight is not the limit, of course. This *plateau* shares little resemblance to the common American "captain's platter" that usually features deep-fried, sometimes batter-encrusted shellfish and flounder alongside Dixie cups brimming with tartar sauce. I admit it, though: I loved the captain's platter when I was a kid and probably still would.

Whenever I see a *plateau de fruits de mer,* I'm reminded of the Dutch still-life masters capturing heaps of seafood with spectacular precision. The message inherent in the paintings, the ephemeral nature of bodily pleasures, can be lost in the viewer's admiration for their exquisite realism. One of the advantages of living in Paris is that you can stroll over to the Louvre and consult these works with your own eyes. The Richelieu wing has rooms dedicated to sixteenth- and seventeenth-century northern European painting. Of all ingredients, I notice that still-life paintings most often feature oysters.

There is no time better to visit a European art museum than in the "r" month of January, and I wanted to see for myself just what was going on with the Dutch artists and their singular obsession with oysters. At one point I wrote to Gereons, a food writer and chef, to ask what the oyster represented to his country's Golden Age still-life painters. He responded immediately, saying that people believed oysters possessed aphrodisiac powers and thus symbolically represented fertility and prosperity.

"Rendering oysters was a bit naughty," he added, "since they stood for sexual freedom in a time when Calvinism was sweeping the Netherlands."

Certainly, the suggestive form of oysters contributes to their sexual insinuations. In Jan Steen's *Girl Eating Oysters,* an attractive young woman looks coquettishly at the viewer with an alluring smile while offering an opened oyster. Still, as far as oysters and eroticism are concerned, hardly any rendition can surpass the Japanese film *Tampopo.* The insinuation is so strong it is comical: a virgin pearl diver feeds an oyster to a gangster out of the palm of her hand after he cuts his lip on the shell. The result is a kiss with a touch of blood.

Oysters possessed other symbolic meanings for the Golden Age Dutch. They represented taste, sensuality, and the temporary pleasures of earthly existence. They are often featured in the still lifes known as *vanitas*—a lush cornucopia of foods, some barely eaten, half-finished glasses of wine, a lemon with its rind peeled in a spiral signifying the unraveling of time, all bathed in a beauteous light that glints off silver, pewter, glass, and perfect pools of oyster liquor.

While these paintings are stunning, I study them for another reason: the oysters don't look anything like the ones my father, brother, and I collected while I grew up in New England, nor do they look like the most common oysters in France. France has been famed since Roman times as Europe's greatest oyster producer. Clearly, the seventeenth-century oysters in these paintings were rounder and flatter than the typical *creuses* that are consumed worldwide.

Mary and I have spent time in Le Pouldu in Brittany, where Gauguin and the impressionists painted. The one oyster in France that seems esteemed above all others, meaning also the most expensive, is the belon, coming from the estuaries of the Belon River. This contributed to my fascination with original native oysters that appear in paintings.

The Neanderthals ate the original flat European oysters, I assume, with more pleasure than many of the foods available to them. These oysters would cost a fortune in any restaurant today, especially when they've been exported. Through the ages, oyster shells have been fashioned into tools, jewelry, and false teeth; ground up for mortar; and pulverized for biomineralization to relieve osteoporosis. The oysters themselves provide zinc, iron, selenium, and vitamin B12, making them nature's depression-fighting food. They contain the whole alphabet of vitamins as well as iodine, calcium, phosphorous, magnesium, and copper, all contributing to general nutrition and bolstering the immune system. And of course there are those omega-3 fatty acids. What the Dutch and just about everyone else claim about oysters being an aphrodisiac enjoys support from scientific studies on amino acids, specifically D-aspartic acid and N-methyl-D-aspartate. No wonder Henry VIII held oyster orgies, Napoleon consumed them before battles, Voltaire and Rousseau ate them for inspiration, and Casanova enjoyed passing one between his lips and those of his lovers. Oysters also figure prominently in the "Party Girl Diet" of recent times. There is a saying that if you drink whiskey with oysters, they turn to cement in your stomach. I am happy to report from experience that this doesn't happen.

I've always adored oysters, and now I find myself living in a truly oyster-crazed country. Oysters in France come in all sizes and from a variety of locales—most notably in the areas between Normandy and the Aquitaine: Isigny, Cancale, Belon, Bourneuf, Marennes-Oléron, and Arcachon, each boasting the perfect sweet-water-meeting-saline conditions for production of the most delectable specimens. The French devour tons of oysters over Christmas and New Year's, when 70 percent of the annual harvest is eaten. A good many oyster lovers spend the holidays with gastroenteritis, but usually, rather than blaming a bad oyster, they attribute it to an unfortunate phenomenon, holiday bad luck.

In the service of research on the genuine European oysters—the ones in the *vanitas* paintings urging us to indulge in earthly sensual pleasures while we still have the chance—I visit most of the major oyster-growing areas in France, including the mucky tidal estuary of the Belon River on the southern side of Brittany's Finistere, where Paul Gauguin once painted land- and seascapes. Gauguin also produced still lifes with oysters, and again the oysters resemble the original flat European variety, which many connoisseurs consider to be the ultimate oyster. They are now raised in the United States, where they are prized for their meaty texture and the savor of sea and minerals.

While researching *huîtres plates* (*Ostrea edulis*), also known as belons, I discover a shocking relative, the wildest of all wild oysters, called a *pied-de-cheval,* or literally "horse's foot," which makes me wonder, given quahog clams with the same nomination, how many things in the world are named after a horse's foot. While sharing an uncanny round appearance, these oysters grow wider than a horse's hoof. They can weigh as much as three pounds and live for thirty years or more. This enormous rare oyster found in Normandy's Bay of Mont Saint-Michel is a specialty of certain restaurants. One large *pied-de-cheval* equals three or four good-sized oysters. Most people, including the French, have never heard of them.

I watch an interview about cooking *pieds-de-cheval* with Olivier Roellinger, whose personal life could make an inspiring movie. In his early twenties, he was beaten nearly to death with a steel bar by five adolescents, lapsed into a coma, recovered, and remade his life to become one of France's greatest chefs. Roellinger doesn't describe the overall sensation of eating the oysters but instead discusses three parts of the anatomy of the *pied-de-cheval* as if each were a remarkable wine. This is an oyster that is perfectly equilibrated for flavor, he maintains. The liver is soft, creamy, and sweet; the foot is muscular, musty, and chewy, with fine, long-lasting flavor; and the mantle, the tissue at the lip of the oyster, is pleasantly bitter. Roellinger, who built his reputation on local ingredients and a comprehensive knowledge of Indian spices, prepares the enormous oyster by cooking it very delicately until it's tepid and then adding what seems to be a few Brussels sprout leaves and a curry cream sauce.

While *pieds-de-cheval* are enormous, much larger oysters exist. Record-sized oysters weighing in at more than eight pounds have been found in the Chesapeake Bay and in waters near Humboldt, California. These behemoths conjure images of an oyster truly large enough for Aphrodite, the love goddess whose name is the root for "aphrodisiac," to have been conceived in.

My favorite oysters are largish but not huge, just a perfect mouthful. But the *pied-de-cheval* is an oddity that intrigues me so much that I organize a trip to the Bay of Mont Saint-Michel just to see if I can find one. I pack the canoe in the trunk along with its Yamaha motor and heavy battery.

The fact is that I have no idea what I'm doing. It's not like you can just dig these things up, or find them stuck to a rock somewhere, or spot them in the water from the canoe. They live in the middle of the English Channel (or La Manche, depending on your national perspective). However, I hike the shores above Granville, a major fishing port, and find shells from *pieds-de-cheval* everywhere, along with an enormous array of wild edibles.

I see clam diggers more than a mile out on surreal stretches of sand, their dogs loping free in long, elliptical orbits.

No one from the fishing fleet in Granville seems to sell *pieds-de-cheval,* so I drive past Mont Saint-Michel and cross into Brittany, arriving at Cancale on the western shore of the bay. Cancale is one of France's most famous producers of oysters, and sure enough, on the north side of the port, at least eight stands are not just selling the bivalves but also opening them for whole families, who sit along the boat ramp happily eating dozens raw for lunch. It's as if I have been transported to the nineteenth century, when families habitually strolled to the port to snack on oysters. The shore is littered with squeezed lemons.

An uncommonly large, ruggedly handsome vendor with black hair displays a crate of the unmistakable *pieds-de-cheval.* I can't believe my luck and ask, "How much are these?"

"Four euros."

"Each?" Even if it equals several of its lesser cousins, the rare oyster seems expensive.

"Okay, I'll take one. How should I cook it?"

"Cook it? Oh no, you don't cook these. That's criminal. Here, I'll open it for you," he offers. "Don't put even a drop of lemon on it. It must be eaten just as is. Nothing is better," he assures me.

A big man like him might be able to eat a pound of oyster in a gulp, but I'm taken aback. I stop him from opening it. "I will take it with me. I want my wife to taste it, too." I walk with the oyster in hand feeling like a Greek discus thrower. In the afternoon, I pick up Mary at the St. Malo train station, and we head for Brittany to enjoy the weekend by the sea and to try out the canoe in the Bay of Morlaix. Once in the car, I introduce Mary to my oyster, and she is suitably shocked.

"He's huge! And so beautiful. Where did you find him?"

"Him?" Author M. F. K. Fisher points out in *Consider the Oyster* that oysters have a peculiar habit of switching sexes, so one can never be sure of the gender. I settle on "it" instead.

"I didn't find it. I bought it," I confess, knowing it's a bit of a letdown.

Mary is more than happy to admire the oyster with me, but has no intention of putting any of it in her mouth, which is odd for a New Orleans girl who grew up amid a cult of oyster consumption. I debate whether I should put my *pied-de-cheval* back in the sea or eat it raw to understand the savors and textures of the different parts. It travels with me for three days, refrigerator hopping, until we arrive in Paris; the oyster's fate is sealed. I set it on the counter, and each time I walk into the room it clamps shut, making the prospect of butchering the oyster all the more painful. Mary is appalled by the thought that it has become a kind of companion.

I down a glass of Muscadet for nerve, reflect on the Dutch paintings and *vanitas* while guessing at the oyster's age. Maybe thirty? Certainly neither Henry VIII nor Napoleon would hesitate to eat this creature, though "Party Girls" might. I quickly cut the abductor muscle, and the *pied-de-cheval* soon lies open, exposing liver, gills, and mantle along with the rest of its nutritious anatomy. I honor the rare oyster and eat the creature raw.

Okay, the wildest wild oyster lives fully up to its billing as a delicacy, just as the vendor in Cancale had promised. Regret strikes almost immediately—not that I had just devoured a companion, but that I didn't buy more *pieds-de-cheval* to experiment with. Two conflicting ideas capture my imagination—my initiator's advocacy of the unadorned and my growing obsession with Roellinger, a former Michelin three-star chef and a Commandeur de l'ordre des Arts et des Lettres. Certainly one wonders if the American Academy of Arts and Letters will recognize chefs as artists one day. Sadly, Roellinger was obliged to relinquish his three-star restaurant at only fifty-three, unable to continue physically. Roellinger inspires me, and, determined to experiment, I find among a plethora of oyster distributors in Paris one that specializes in Cancale oysters, a place that promisingly call itself Pleine Mer. It happens to be across town from us, and I'm on the phone in no time.

"You list *pieds-de-cheval.* Do you have them right now?" "No, we only get them from time to time."

"Oh, what times are those?"

"Special times."

"Can they be ordered?"

"Oh, yes, I can have them for you by Thursday."

I begin to see how "special times" works.

"I want two, your biggest."

The Pleine Mer, a seemingly modest place, serves as both an oyster restaurant and vendor, like many oyster bars in Paris. Oyster restaurants in our neighborhood tend to be a bit pretentious and overpriced, though admittedly you can compare an impressive array of oyster types matched to various wines—a marriage of wine bar and oyster bar serving up beautiful chemical sensations for your oral cavity. When I arrive at the Pleine Mer, a friendly, wiry-looking guy with salt-and-pepper hair seems happy to see me, as if he knows me. He explains that the oyster boat that rakes the sea bottom in the Bay of Mont Saint-Michel couldn't get out because of a malfunctioning lock in the harbor.

"A malfunctioning lock?" I am incredulous.

"Next Tuesday I will have two large *pieds-de-cheval* for you," he promises, leaving me with the impression that the boat would go to sea specifically for my two oysters.

When I return on Thursday to the Pleine Mer on my way to work, I feel as if I have a brother. "They are *exceptionnelles,*" he assures me, removing them from his cold storage. He charges me an astounding twenty euros, ten euros each. So much for brotherhood. Grumpily, I wonder if they might not have been cheaper at Roellinger's three-star restaurant.

I confess that I'm also slightly disappointed because they are a few centimeters smaller than my first one. At work, I pull them out of the blue plastic bag full of seaweed that the vendor packed to keep them fresh, and hand the remarkable discs around for inspection.

"They look like actual horse's hooves, don't they?"

My colleagues agree politely, but with somewhat less enthusiasm.

My mother nails a recipe for the dish after I show her a video of Roellinger at work. She knows about cooking oysters only until tepid, the delicacy of cream sauce, and the nuances of curry, sharing the great chef's passion for exotic flavoring and his interest in the history of the spice trade.

The wildest wild oyster is all the more impressive when one considers the numerous oyster cultivators in France producing for consumers worldwide. The native oysters like belons are highly prized, which is reflected in their price, often double that of any on display around them. The available species have changed a good deal in recent decades, as cultivators have been forced to introduce foreign species resistant to diseases that crop up.

One Sunday in September Mary, her niece Margie, and I, traveling

Madame Diégues holding *pieds-de-cheval* from Cancale (Paris)

coastal areas of western France, decide to stop to picnic on the beach with a broad view of L'Ile d'Oréron across the straits near the mouth of the Seudre River. Anyone viewing the area from a satellite would be astonished by the size of the extensive and intricate matrix of marsh channels and rectangular pools for oyster farming. The Marennes-Oléron in the Department Charente-Maritime is the largest oyster-farming region in Europe, producing sixty thousand metric tons of *fines de claire,* oysters that have been matured in salt ponds called *claire.* Much table salt comes from this area, too. The area was attractive to wealthy Roman families, whose history of oyster farming goes back nearly to the time of Christ. No less a personage than Pliny kept his own *ostrearum vivarium* for "fattening" oysters after travel. In fact, the Romans set up a series of vivariums on routes from Britain and France to keep them fresh during transport. They were also transported by cart in winter, as Seamus Heaney describes in his poem "Oysters":

> Over the Alps, packed deep in hay and snow,
> The Romans hauled their oysters south to Rome:
> I saw damp panniers disgorge
> The frond-lipped, brine-stung
> Glut of privilege

Although it is a Sunday, we decide to explore the *claires,* and happen upon an oyster farmer who is happy to talk to us about the intricacies of raising his particular kind of livestock. For example, time spent in the basins and oyster density are what distinguish *fines de claire* from the more expensive *spéciales.* Key qualities include uniform shape, fresh sea odor, and saline balance. One elusive element is the green or blue gills that gleam like jade. He tells us in detail about the progression of oyster diseases that spread from native varieties to Portuguese and, more recently, Japanese oysters. The Japanese, or Pacific version now suffers from oyster herpes, a rampant virus some blame on global warming. The disease leaves farmers searching for alternative sources of income, among them raising hardy imperial prawns in their basins. Oysters are often placed in mesh sacks for final cleaning in open waters. The oyster farmer shows us a sack of dead oysters, a poignant example of disease.

The eastern oyster, a true North American native of the Eastern Seaboard, is famously coveted from the Chesapeake Bay, New York Harbor, Long Island Sound, and on up to Maine. It has suffered primarily from overharvesting and pollution. A few centuries ago, oysters grew so thick in the Chesapeake Bay that they formed shoals, presenting hazards to the likes of Captain John Smith when he navigated the estuary. During a time of drought and starvation in Jamestown, Smith ordered his men to live by the riverside in order to survive on oysters. The drought changed the saline content of the James River, permitting oysters to grow upstream from the Chesapeake Bay closer to the Virginia Colony. Today, the oyster population in the bay area is only 1 percent of what it was in Smith's time.

One learns to appreciate all the more the native oyster survivors and the truly wild oyster, how they made their way into still-life painting, the challenge of rendering their silver-gray color, the light reflected off their liquor, their sensual suggestiveness, the wine in the accompanying glass, the tears on the lemon, all conspiring against depression. One question still lingers, however: How did the great painters resist simply gulping their models down?

5

DRINKING CUP OF THE GODS

TRACKING DOWN THE *pied-de-cheval* reignites my childhood passion for collecting shellfish and reading shorelines to discover what clings and hides there, sifting the estuaries, bays, and open waters. After my parents divorced, money became even tighter than before, but my brother and I knew we could supply meals, thanks to the skills Dad had honed in us. In my preadolescent mind, gathering wild edibles took on a heroic aura: here we were, providing for our single-mother tribe. In Rhode Island, my brother and I took paths through hedges of tough rugosa roses, which were resistant to salt, down to the rocky shore of a small inlet where we stored our gear in a washed-up boat hull. Here we'd dive for fish. At low tide, we'd go to the salt-pond clam beds at Ninigret, Quonochontaug, and Winnapaug, names derived from the language of the original people who had lived there: Wampanoag, Niantics, and Narragansetts.

We used our bare feet to probe for quahogs, or poquauhock—"horse fish," so called because of the shape of the shell, perhaps. The Latin name is more interesting: *mercenaria,* or related to commerce. Indeed, the shells, particularly the blue portion, were used to make wampum beads and jewelry.

One learns quickly that detecting clams in lagoon muck by feeling for them is not for the faint of heart. This is the art of sensation—a squish between the toes, and then the familiar feel of the siphon edge of a clam—but we experienced regular detonations of adrenalin when stepping on eels, flatfish, the claws of a blue crab, or, God forbid, an oyster toadfish sporting poisonous spines. These creatures, so ugly as to be comical-looking, are capable of making loud, foghorn-like sounds both underwater and above it. I've also had the unpleasant experience of having one rocket out of a discarded can into my face, the ultimate jack-in-the-box surprise.

Even with so much experience gathering mollusks and crustaceans, my entry into the world of *pêche à pied* in France was somewhat timid. After all, the coastline was new to me, as were some of the gathering methods, rules, and the collectible creatures themselves. The crabs are different, the three main edible ones being a *crabe torteau* (brown crab) that can weigh as much as six pounds, *crabe-araignée* (European spider crab), and the feisty little *étrille* (velvet swimmer crab). The French make bisques and sauces out of their native European green crabs, extraordinary pesky survivors that are considered a nightmarish invasive species elsewhere, particularly the American Northeast. These pinching sea crustaceans were once heaped together with lobsters and langoustines, as Charles Dickens describes in *David Copperfield,* "in a state of wonderful conglomeration with one another, and never leaving off pinching whatever they laid hold of"—clearly the result of crab-panic from battling people and each other for self-preservation.

I'm most familiar with blue crabs, although when I lived in San Francisco I developed a great appreciation for the local Dungeness crabs. The blue crab's Achilles' heel, so to speak, benefits the common crabber. Its survival-of-the-fittest aggressive instinct translates into the biggest crab chasing the smallest ones off a fish head on a string, sealing its own fate when the tug-of-war ends with a scoop net. Blue crabs are common down the entire East Coast, Maryland in particular boasting of its Chesapeake Bay crabs, which are served boiled or in sliders or salads. Truth be told, however, 80 percent of the crabs served in Maryland restaurants come from Louisiana, the true American blue-crab capital.

More advanced "interoceanic transport" started bringing the American blue crab and other creatures to the Mediterranean in the 1940s in an early wave of bioinvasions. The blue crab began appearing in Egyptian, Italian, and Israeli coastal waters and eventually made its way into the Black Sea. Scientists have been trapping and measuring American blues in Italy's Acquatina lagoon and Torre Colimena basin, and the crabs are now showing up in Albania's Adriatic waters as well.

I am surprised to find blue crabs in markets in Paris's two Chinatowns.

Four-pound brown crab from Brittany (Paris)

Asians crave crab for their traditional cuisine, calling a similar-looking native species, *Portunus pelagicus,* "flower crabs" or "beautiful swimmers," I suppose because of the gorgeous sapphire tint of their shells. Conversely, the Asian crab has a wide distribution from Japan through Southeast Asian waters down to Australia and even west to East Africa. While the Spanish and the Greeks raise the Atlantic *Callinectes sapidus* that appear in Paris, *Portunus pelagicus* is appearing in the Mediterranean from the Red Sea via the Suez Canal. They are also colonizing waters off Turkey.

A number of clam species, too, are different in Europe. Perhaps the most coveted are those called *palourdes* in France and crosscut carpet shells in England. The red-and-cream, varnished-looking *amandes de mer* (almonds of the sea) sound much more appealing than the British "dog cockle," though they're the same thing; *Coques commons,* a hunter-gatherer staple, are among the easiest to find. *Praire,* thick, white-shelled clams with a rough surface, are often found raw in *plateaux de fruits de mer.* The smallest clams, with colorful shells of yellow, purple, orange, or red, are hardly an inch long, and are called *Donax truncalus, donax* meaning "beautiful thing." They are common on broad, sandy beaches in the littoral zone and move from one position to the next by pushing themselves about with their tiny, nearly transparent siphons in what's called "the dance of the coquinas." The French call these clams *tellines,* and in

Italy they are known as *arsella.* They are used in soups, pasta, and risotto dishes. In Spain, *almejas coquinas* are cooked classically with butter, garlic, olive oil, parsley, and white wine for tapas.

The clam can't boast quite the same level of sexual symbolism as the oyster in still-life painting, though Georgia O'Keeffe's *Slightly Opened Clam Shell* offers a stirring argument to the contrary. Clams tend to find their way into more tranquil seashore landscapes populated by small groups or solitary clam diggers, a step out of *vanitas* into romantic merging with nature.

While it is often said that Venus was born in an oyster or a clam, Botticelli's iconic *Birth of Venus* clearly shows her as a fully mature, natural redhead emerging from the sea on a scallop shell. Shall we just say that the seashell in antiquity was a symbol of flowering? Sea scallops in France are called *coquilles Saint Jacques,* the shell being the symbol of Saint James the Greater, one of the twelve apostles. Many legends link Saint James to scallops. According to one, Saint James saves a drowning Spanish nobleman, who emerges from the Spanish north shore covered in scallops, leading to the nobleman's conversion. In another, Saint James's body somehow washes up on the Spanish coast covered in scallops. The scallop shell became an emblem on shields of certain crusaders and a religious talisman for the pilgrimage to Santiago de Compostela, one of the major routes starting in Vézelay, near our country home. Whatever the case, it's impossible to overstate the appreciation of *coquilles Saint Jacques* in France. However, the *plateau de fruits de mer,* a shrine to shelled sea creatures, rarely features them. Instead, they find themselves on the menus of the most refined restaurants as a challenge to the world's greatest cooks to enhance their firm texture and sweet, light flavor.

In America, the sea scallop is rarely presented with its coral, or roe. Mary recalls seeing fishermen clean scallops on the shore of Nantucket, making one pile of the prized nut (white muscle) and the other of orange coral, which was then tossed to ecstatic swooping gulls. This sort of waste would shock most French connoisseurs. I always associate Nantucket with the best bay scallops anywhere. I remember the owner of my favorite fish market in Connecticut picking up a clean white bucket with the freshest cleaned Nantucket bay scallops and saying, "Go ahead, taste these. It's okay, eat them just as they are." It was the first time I'd ever eaten scallops raw, and I have loved making scallop *carpaccio* ever since, though with the larger sea scallops available in France. I also make scallop ceviche, a seemingly simple cold Latin American dish that actually requires great care if one is not to overwhelm the delicate flavor of the scallops with the lime juice that "cooks" them. In the States, both sea and bay scallops are generally sold shucked, whereas in France they are offered alive in their shells. The clapping shells are weighed—along with any attendant seaweed, limpets, and barnacles—and sold by the kilo. It's always a bit disconcerting afterward, when the pulsing white muscle and coral have been extracted, to see how disproportionate they are to the tossed-out waste you've just paid for.

One early autumn, when Mary's niece Margie was visiting from Texas, we decided to take her to a bed-and-breakfast on the Bay of Morlaix. The three of us strolled along the shoreline after the great tide receded, leaving behind it pools filled with shrimp, crabs, snails, mussels, oysters, and small fish darting amid the dulse and rockweed. Margie and Mary, scavenging ahead of me, brought back an assortment of lovely shells, stones, and small, panicked crabs. I was especially struck by the sheer quantity and size of the limpets, dozens to a rock, some as large as the old half-dollar. You will not find these cap-shaped Chinese limpets on your *plateau de fruits de mer,* nor will they appear in the paintings of Jan de Heem or Wellem Kalf.

"What do you think of these things?" I ask.

"They're cool," Mary responds. "They go around cleaning up slime from rocks."

"They move?"

"Sure, on their stomachs. You know—gastropods, from the Greek," she adds, a bit pedantically. "*Gastro,* stomach. *Pod,* foot."

"Are they edible?"

"Edible? You want to eat limpets?"

"Well, what if you're starving to death?" I persist.

Farther down the beach, we encounter Madame Guillou, owner of our bed-and-breakfast. "What are those little Chinese cap–like creatures clinging to rocks? We call them limpets in English."

"We say '*patelles*'—cups of the gods."

"Are they edible?"

"Of course, we locals do so. When I was a girl, we would collect them on Sunday and serve them as a part of our large family meal."

In the States, unless you are from Hawaii, you don't hear much about eating limpets. The common New England tortoise-shell limpets just seem too small to consider eating, though if you were desperate enough, the slipper-shell limpets that cluster on top of each other might be a different story.

We had planned the journey in part to try out our canoe in the Bay of Morlaix, with the objective of finding relatively untouched spots to collect mussels and other seafood. For Margie, a nature writer and painter, canoeing and kayaking have become second nature, a convenient way of exploring large portions of major Texas rivers, so I was keen to learn from her. The three of us arrived at a boat launch at high tide. We inflated the canoe, attached the motor, and were cruising away from shore when the left back air chamber began to soften. Weighed down by three people, a motor, and a battery, the canoe began sinking rapidly and soon looked like a doomed moth struggling on water. Once back on shore, Margie gave a quick diagnosis, pointing out bubbling abrasions. Unfazed, she marked the holes, and later patched them expertly.

On returning to Paris, I began researching limpets, watching them zoom around, cleaning off rocks, in time-lapse films. One marine biologist studying their territorial behavior described them running into each other like bumper cars, with the smaller ones reversing away at top (limpet) speed. I ran across a recent BBC headline that proclaimed, "Limpet Teeth Set New Strength Record," accompanied by a microscope image suggesting that if a limpet were large enough it would terrify a great white shark. Limpet teeth protrude from their tongues, and the mineral-protein composite in limpets' teeth has now replaced the spider web as the strongest-known natural substance.

A video on YouTube shows two adolescent girls plucking limpets out of their shells and popping them in their mouths raw. With big smiles, they toss the shells over their shoulders. In the Pico Azores, such enthusiasm is shown for *lapas*—as limpets, both raw and cooked, are called in Portuguese—that limits are set on how many a person can collect. In many countries, scruffy survivalists knock limpets off rocks and roast them upside down over open fires. Although it seems odd that survivalists post videos on YouTube, they make snacking on limpets seem appealing.

"I'm going to try them," I tell Mary. "After all, Neanderthals and Paleolithic *Homo sapiens* ate them."

"Yeah, but we have a *choice,*" she replies pointedly. She'd recently read in John Wright's *Edible Seashore* that "anyone who enjoys eating pencil rubbers dipped in fish paste will find the common limpet a treat."

"What about the Festa da Lapa in the Azores, where they feast on limpets for three days while guzzling beer? Or the Hawaiian opihi limpets going for eighteen dollars a pound in the market? They're just snails," I argue. "You love *bigorneaux,* right?" The French are great consumers of *bulots* and the smaller *bigorneaux*—common periwinkles, a species introduced to America that now seems to cover every rock and piling. They use sewing pins to remove the trapdoor and extract the little snail, which is coiled like a spring and has a livery taste. Both can be found alive—*vivant*—or precooked in almost every fish shop in the country, and while I never ate sea snails in the States, save *scungilli* (a slightly repulsive word) in Italian restaurants, I am fond of their chewy texture and delicate flavor, peppery from their cooking bouillon (similar to crab boil) and dipped in house-made mayonnaise. But enthusiastic limpet consumption appears to be more specialized according to place and cultural acceptance. My Scottish friend Geoff Gilbert recalls his father on Whalsay popping them in his mouth like chewing gum. In the taste-of-place spirit, limpet chewing gum seems fitting in the sub-Arctic Circle Shetlands.

With various limpet-consumption traditions in mind, I remain unconvinced that the creatures will taste like fishy pencil erasers. In the world of *pêche à pied,* there is a gastropod that shares a remarkable number of similarities with limpets, but is so sought after that in some parts of the world overfishing has brought it to the brink of extinction. Abalone, it turns out, are native to France and Brittany in particular. They are known here as *ormeau,* a word derived from the Latin *Auris maris*—"ear of the sea."

It's easy to imagine abalone possessing mythic qualities. Don't kids wonder what mermaids eat? I pose the question to Amanda, our evidence-based-medicine friend at Oxford, who comes every summer to Rogny. She

Stuart Dischell collecting limpets
(Anse du Guesclin, Brittany)

reports, "Mermaids require the crazed love of seduced sailors to sustain and nourish themselves." This rings true enough, and sometimes overly zealous mermaids tragically drown the very sailors they are trying to seduce. They don't mean to, necessarily.

Clearly, though, mermaids are mammals, so might they not eat abalone and seaweed? Mermaids and abalone evoke the Japanese ama divers, "sea women" wearing only *fundoshis,* loincloths, and plunging to depths of up to 70 feet for lobsters, urchins, octopuses, seaweed, and, most famously, pearl oysters. (The last-named is actually a kind of sea clam and not an oyster at all.) The ama tradition is two thousand years old, and the great eighteenth-century woodblock print artists, including Utamaro and Hokusai, rendered them gorgeously, their hair undulating in the water as they collect their prey amid coral and sponges, their entourage waiting ashore with baskets. Sometimes the prints are fanciful, and the ama divers, the real mermaids, must fearlessly battle underwater dragons, or encounter sea ghosts.

Awabi—abalone—divers are also women, and some woodblock prints, particularly those of Hokusai, depict them carrying baskets heavily laden with gastropod treasure, dragging masses of fresh seaweed to the water's edge. These images alone convince me—a certified diver myself since age eleven—that if diving were considered an art, the sea women would be its masters.

I knew of abalone as a kid growing up in New England only through its oval dome-shaped shell, pocked with a series of respiration holes, or pores. It's widely known that abalone produces nacre on the inside of the shell, giving it a dazzling iridescence and making it a source for mother of pearl. The abalone excretes layers of nacre to create a smooth, durable surface to protect its soft tissue from rough debris and parasites. The nacre is composed of aragonite platelets that refract light, producing glints of green, pink, red, blue, and silver. While the abalone shell is highly valued for making jewelry, decorating musical instruments, and creating eye-catching buttons, the animal's meaty foot is also treasured around the world as a wild edible.

When I moved to northern California in my late twenties, I often watched abalone divers in the famed Red Triangle, an area bordered by Bodega Bay to the north, the Fallon Islands to the west, and Big Sur to the south. It is a zone particularly rich in both abalone and great white sharks, which probably explains the mildly bloody-sounding name. Myths abound, one being that abalone emit a shark-attracting charge when pried off rocks with an "ab bar." The prospect of shark attacks does add a certain frisson to the challenge of abalone harvesting, but in reality they rarely pose a problem. Nevertheless, abalone diving has developed into an extreme sport because divers are not allowed to use air tanks. There is too much poaching, and I well know the advantage the tanks offer. However, the rough Pacific waters and their currents north of San Francisco present the most serious dangers. Divers are dashed on rocks, trapped in caves, or become entangled in abalone's favorite health food—huge, caramel-colored ribbons of kelp. While California coastal rangers find bodies washed up regularly, the danger attracts characters who feel the need to test themselves against the sea. Diver safety represents only one concern for the rangers; they contend with rampant poaching, with a pound of abalone commanding prices up to one hundred dollars.

Remarkably, seven species of abalone are found in California, varying in size, number of respiratory pores, and habitat: tidal or subtidal, and at depths ranging from 0 to 120 feet. Except for pinto and flat abalone, they are named by color: black, red, pink, green, and white, all edible. Even while I was living in San Francisco, abalone diving was highly restricted. Once considered dirt-cheap seafood, abalone became overfished in the 1950s as a highly prized export to Asia. Other connoisseurs include crabs, lobsters, bat rays, octopuses, various fish, and even predatory snails. Perhaps the best diver of all, the sea otter, gathers abalone all too efficiently, floating blissfully on its back and clutching the delicacy to its chest as if it were a jewel box.

Before I'd ever eaten abalone, I harbored the negative impression that it was overly tough, but also the positive one that it might taste something like *scungilli.* I consumed my first abalone in San Francisco's Chinatown and was unimpressed, probably because abalone is often mixed with other foods such as chicken, beef, or eggs, and frequently comes out of a can. Perhaps there is a synergy of flavors, particularly with eggs, but to me the other ingredients mask the flavor. I had abalone again in Houston, Texas, at a starred Asian restaurant where diners had private walled-in cubicles. I remember well the sensation of being, as the French say, *renversé*—knocked over by the delicate richness and meaty texture.

During the course of my limpet experiments, I discovered that *ormeaux* production in France has become so successful that they're now for sale in our country supermarkets, so I bought one to test at home. Neither my mother nor Mary had ever tasted abalone before, so all three of us went about researching how to shuck, clean, and cook it. We huddled and debated until at last we agreed to prepare it in the simplest, purest fashion possible in order to immerse ourselves in the essence of its flavor.

I prepped myself to butcher my first abalone by watching a half-dozen video demonstrations. Somehow I thought abalone were headless creatures, like clams and oysters, but abalone do have heads with eerie blue, somewhat slanted eyes that I found, and continue to find, most unsettling. After shucking the body out of its stunning shell, I immediately beheaded it and removed the organs, leaving the disproportionately large and muscular foot. This foot creates suction so that abalone can cling to rocks, but its mobility, which is extremely limited, comes from *epipodium,* small tentacles and sensory tissue at the foot's edge. Once I had trimmed the blackish rim away, I was left with an ivory-colored oval of firm meat, something like a bar of Dove hand soap. I sliced it in half, making two ministeaks, smacked them a couple of times with the flat of a cleaver, and flash-sautéed them in an olive oil/butter combination. Mary remarked that it tasted like veal; my mother was very taken with its sweetness and firm yet tender texture.

Enthralled with our abalone inauguration, I bought four more the next day, and with each one we tried a different recipe: a panko-breaded abalone sauté served on artichoke hearts; an abalone ceviche; a delicate celery and abalone Chinese stir-fry; and abalone sashimi with seaweed salad. All these dishes have their merits, although the results for the ceviche were the most disappointing. "Cooking" with lime juice made the abalone tough and dominated its flavor. Serving creatures accompanied by the things that they eat intrigues me, and in the case of abalone, that means seaweed. Abalone sashimi with seaweed salad was exquisite, perfect beauty food for ama divers and mermaids alike.

As the beginning of autumn rolled around—along with abalone season—I spontaneously decided to take my mother to the Brittany shore for a few days. There, I knew, peace would wash over her like a narcotic, and I would see the expression I remembered so well from when she was a young mother staring off for hours at the sea. Less altruistically, I also harbored the fantasy that I might find, at the deepest ebb of low tide, an abalone in the wild. My mother hardly noticed when I'd disappear among the rocks, taking hard falls on rockweed and kelp. And as fate would have it, I found everything but abalone.

Nevertheless, we discovered that an Australian had created a thriving abalone farm called France Haliotis at the far northern tip of Finistère. We visited the farm and saw cement basins with fresh flowing seawater and large plastic crates, some being raised on a forklift, and wheeled from the edge of the marsh to a basin. A young aqua farmer explained, "We grow abalone from three to five years old by stuffing it on kelp inside of these plastic crates, which are dropped into the open ocean. Ten to fifteen pounds of kelp equal one pound of abalone, so the kelp has to be recharged from time to time. We farm the seaweed, too, to maintain a renewable harvest."

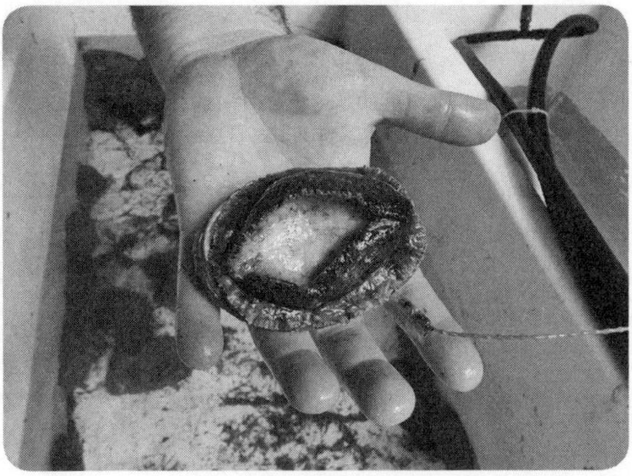

Abalone at France Haliotis
(Plouguerneau, Brittany)

The farmer showed us several basins, each one holding dozens of retail-ready abalone attached to the bottom and sides. The disparity in the size was notable: one vat was filled with abalone as small as three inches in diameter; another with creatures the size of a mango.

"What's the difference here?" I asked.

"The small ones are ours, the farmed ones. These larger ones were gathered by divers."

"They're wild?"

"Yes, and considerably cheaper."

"I would have expected the opposite. Wild equals more flavor, right?"

"Not according to the connoisseurs," he assured me.

Reaching into the tank filled with wild abalone, he pulled out one, extended it toward us, and turned it over in his palm while the turquoise-blue rim of the foot curled like petals. Hiroshige's great abalone print from his series called *Fish Subjects* captures this beautifully, and I pondered what Georgia O'Keeffe might have done with this color and form. My mother sorted through the collection of nacre jewelry, and I bought jars of abalone *rillettes,* really just a terrine of abalone and dulse, another culinary synergy between the creature and what it eats.

We left France Haliotis with our purchases and drove down the coast.

"Let's cook limpets on the beach like survivalists do," I suggested.

I had brought along a small sauté pan, some oil, and matches. By the time we arrived at the beach, I saw that my mother had slipped into the sort of dreamy reverie that invariably seizes her at the seashore. Gradually it came to me—almost a revelation—that with the mussel beds, limpets, periwinkles, seaweed, seaside vegetation, and more in that very spot, we could find enough food to survive handsomely just by gathering.

"Why don't I barbecue some mussels over coals?" I offered. My mother, however, remained distracted.

"Maybe I'll cook some limpets, too. What do you think?"

Nothing. My mother doesn't hear well.

"Limpets," I tried one more time, rather loudly.

"They sound too friendly," my mother said.

6

THE GOOSE TREE

WHAT IF THERE WERE a wild goose species that never made a nest, but just appeared out of nowhere each summer? How would you explain that if you didn't know about migration? Jehan de Mandeville tried to elucidate this mystery. In his fourteenth-century book translated as *Travels of Sir John Mandeville,* he claimed that they came from goose trees: "I told them of as great a marvel to them, that is amongst us, and that was of the Bernakes. For I told them that in our country were trees that bear a fruit that become birds flying, and those that fell in the water live, and they that fall on the earth die anon, and they be right good to man's meat." The myth was that this kind of black goose generated from a special barnacle often found on logs or large branches in the open sea. The connection comes because the barnacle has a long, rubbery stalk resembling a gooseneck and shells at the end that look like a goose's head or perhaps a beak. The English call this odd-looking arthropod the gooseneck barnacle. In turn, because superstition had it that these wild geese came from the barnacles, they were named barnacle geese. Both names for these different creatures have stuck to this day. The barnacle is also known as *pouce-pied* in French and *percebe* in Spanish, both meaning "thumb foot."

A remarkable part of the gooseneck barnacle's anatomy includes appendages called "cirri," pairs of fine *rami,* limbs that look like feathers, especially when you look closely at the black bands on gray. These cirri "lasso" and entrap passing nutrients such as algae, larvae, amphipods, even tiny shrimp and clams, and other minute creatures. The cirri's feather-like appearance only enhanced the confusion between goose and barnacle. Because the "geese" presumably came from these natal "thumb feet" growing on submerged trees and the sea, they were considered shellfish, not meat, and therefore could be roasted and happily eaten on Fridays or during Lent.

Nowadays, we've learned to distinguish the two animals as entirely separate beings, although they will be forever linked in name and folklore as barnacles. I had never heard of gooseneck barnacles until, during my reconnaissance of fish markets, I spied some marked only with a price: the euro equivalent of twenty-five dollars a pound. To be honest, they looked revolting. While I was hovering over them, one of the fish sellers approached.

"Have you been served?" she inquired politely.

"What do you call these?"

"*Pouces-pieds.*" Thumb-feet: a genetic disaster. But I could tell from the plates of shell at the end, and the way the creatures had been harvested in clusters that were often still attached to a chip of stone, that they were barnacles.

"Hideous, aren't they?" I commented, with horrified curiosity.

"*Ils sont exquis,*" she replied dispassionately, and turned away for a series of violent sneezes, obviously suffering from a dreadful cold. "Prized in Spain and Portugal," she croaked.

Longtime customers queried with genuine concern, "*Ça va?*"

"Yes, yes, it's okay. Don't worry. They have me on the right antibiotics now." They all nodded and smiled encouragingly.

The word "exquisite" conflicted profoundly with the appearance of the creatures—thick three-inch-long gradient orange-to-black worms with teeth on one end.

Turning back to me, the fish seller asserted, "They are a delicacy. Would you like to try some?"

I stalled.

"How are they prepared?"

"Six minutes in boiling seawater." I assumed she meant salted water since we were in Paris, two hours from the Atlantic. Then she picked up a cluster, pulled off one stalk, held it in her thumb and forefinger in front of me, and with her other hand pinched the claw-like end with a little twist. It's this twist that breaks the claw from the tough tubular jacket so that the meaty stem may be extracted. She demonstrated this in mime, since *pouce-pieds* have to be cooked first or they will be tough as a rubber hose.

Gooseneck barnacles (Rogny-les-Sept-Écluses, Burgundy)

I'm sure this sounds like a cliché, but in France anything can be a delicacy if presented in the right context. The relative affluence of a Parisian neighborhood then dictates everyday outrageous prices.

"Okay, I'll take these," I said, pointing to several of the thickest, freshest-looking clusters, the orange stems almost glowing.

The seller wore no white apron, and her full chest in tight leotard gray heaved as she coughed. I was already regretting my purchase, not just because the barnacles looked like the fingers of a troll and cost a fortune, but also because I imagined spending the next three weeks with pneumonia.

Mary wasn't at the apartment when I came home, but Madame Diégues, our Portuguese friend, came over. Madame Diégues is a small woman in her early sixties, with dark Iberian features, naturally attractive and talkative. She loves to engage me in discussions of food. I was of course anxious to show her that I had bought and would learn to appreciate a delicacy from her home country—the *pouce-pieds,* or *percebes.* (In Portuguese, it's *pedunculata.*) I imagined Madame Diégues providing me with a special authentic recipe. After all, she's always offering me advice on where to shop and what to cook.

Of course, it's true that when I tried to interrogate her about limpets, supposedly so popular in certain Portuguese cuisines, she had no idea what I was talking about. But then Madame Diégues's family lives in the hills near the Spanish border, far from the Azores or the northern coast where such creatures abound. And there is the likelihood that I'm not pronouncing any of the words right, forcing her to knit her eyebrows in perplexed concentration.

I did discover that, while limpets may be alien to the mountains of Portugal, octopus somehow is not. It's a food for celebrations there, at least in Madame Diégues's family, and it was she who taught me how to cook the first one I ever brought home from the market. She saw the octopus brooding in the sink and exclaimed, "*Quelle belle bête!*" She showed me how to remove the beak and ink sacs and clean the suckers that even in death manage to cling unpleasantly to your skin. Madame Diégues often says, "No one wants to touch the earth. That is why everything has lost its flavor." How sensual that seems: touch and flavor, except when it's the clinging sucker of a dead octopus. Madame Diégues simply prepared a court bouillon with a carrot, bay leaf, half an onion, garlic, parsley, and peppercorns.

"Never add salt," she admonished. "It detaches the skin." This must have been the error my father made once when his octopus turned into a pot full of pink, floating flesh.

She lifted the octopus out of the sink, its tentacles drooping more than a half meter long.

"You have to dunk it several times to help make it tender." She held the beast over the large stockpot and began plunging it methodically into the boiling court bouillon. The tentacles instantly came to life, turning purplish and coiling, some form of contraction in the moribund cells. All the while Madame Diégues shrieked out, "Look, I'm a witch! I'm a witch!"

Well, octopus is one thing, but prehistoric-looking *pedunculata, pouce-pieds, percebes* another. Madame Diégues absolutely refused to work her sorcery on gooseneck barnacles, no matter how important touch and taste are to her.

"No, no, I don't know those," she proclaimed, waving her hands in front of her face in disgust.

It never surprises Mary when I bring home unusual foods to try. Just the week before I had purchased sea figs, also known as *Viagra de Marseilles* for their alleged revitalizing powers. On first inspection, they resemble hardened clumps of organic waste, the last thing you would consider

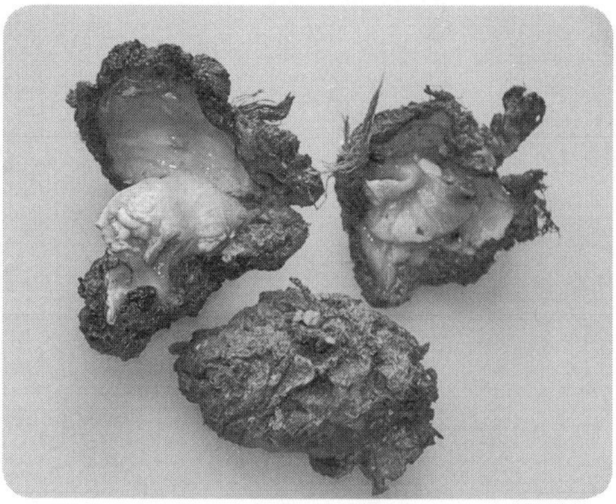

Sea figs (Paris)

edible, but concealed inside is bright orange-and-red flesh that has an intense iodine taste equaling or surpassing that of sea urchins. As primitive as sea figs might appear, they fall under the tunicate classification: marine animals that have a nerve cord and thus are fairly sophisticated on the evolutionary chain despite their blob-like appearance and common name: sea squirts. After trying sea figs, you realize immediately why the ancient Greeks and Romans considered them marine treasures.

When I emptied the bag to show Mary the gooseneck barnacles, I expected her to gasp in horror, as I did myself at the fish store, but I got a different reaction.

"What are they?" she asked, fascinated. "They look like penises with teeth."

"They're a delicacy," I assure her.

Mary inspected one of the toothy worms carefully. "A sessile crustacean, a suspension feeder," she pronounced. "You know, something that traps its food in currents."

"How did you know that?"

Mary launched into a lengthy description of biomorphology.

"Yeah, okay, but would you eat one?"

"Of course."

Gooseneck barnacles have a strong preference for open seas, and grow most commonly where waves crash against rugged rock cliffs in such places as Cornwall, Galicia, and Brittany. Their natural habitat makes them inaccessible to the ordinary forager. They can be found on coasts from the Aleutian Islands down to Chile, and the rough shores of Washington State and British Columbia. Northwest Pacific coastal Indian tribes ate them cooked in ash. These days they're becoming more and more popular for commercial harvesting, to the degree that legal protections are in place in certain areas.

Mary and I agree to preserve their essence by simply boiling them and serving them with butter and toast. One of our most memorable moments on a visit to the southern coast of Australia was pulling into Apollo Bay Fish Fishermen's Co-op just as it was closing and coming out with a prized presteamed spiny lobster. We picked up butter and English muffins at a convenience store and, back in our Best Western kitchenette, dined on hot lobster and English muffins, a delicious combination. A connoisseur would have called us barbarians. You can't get good English muffins in Paris, so we couldn't reproduce our memorable South Australian experience exactly, but we could still approximate it with buttered toast and gooseneck barnacles to get the essence of taste and texture.

Cooking the barnacles did little to improve their nightmarish appearance—those steaming extraterrestrial claws!—but with one twist of the shell tip, the outer sleeve separated and could be easily slipped off, just as the ailing fish seller had demonstrated. Trepidation turned to wonder. How does one put into words what they taste like? The first impression is of a sweet sea flavor similar to that of the meat in lobster legs, but the texture is more like the necks of steamer clams stripped of their sheaths, or cleaned and tender strips of razor clams. The Spanish would call it the pure marine essence of a mermaid's kiss. I've never kissed a mermaid, but I imagine they mean sweet with a hint of sea salt. What else can I say? They were delicious.

Like so many now-treasured seafoods, gooseneck barnacles were originally considered peasant fare, sold after they were scraped off the hulls of ships. Now they find their way onto the menus of top restaurants in New York, Toronto, and Madrid. As a final testament to their rehabilitation, they're beginning to show up in the major French supermarkets.

Mary and I always try to fit in a week by the sea at the beginning of September, just before I have to go back to work and when the major vacation period finishes. Despite the chill at night with the turn of season, the water is still warm enough for swimming. The afternoons are bright and clear, the grasses turning to seed and orchards hung with autumn fruit. This year, we decide to go to Belle Ile for the first time.

I'm trying to think of an American equivalent of Belle Ile, a small island that lies off the southern coast of Brittany near Quiberon and Carnac. This is the land of *dolmens,* megalithic arrangements of enormous stones to honor the dead, and *menhir,* single standing stones or groupings that might have served as territorial markers, celestial calendars, or altars for ceremonies. The reasons for erecting these monoliths, though often guessed at, remain a mystery.

I'd like to say the spleen-shaped Belle Ile reminds me of Nantucket or Martha's Vineyard, but the island is smaller and far more modest economically. Massive glacial movements and rising seas formed Cape Cod, Nantucket, Martha's Vineyard, and the Elizabeth Islands. Belle Ile, on the other hand, broke off from the mainland only about six thousand years ago. Its formation is essentially that of a plateau at sea, with especially dramatic cliffs along the western and southern coastlines. Even where the sea is accessible, it's still necessary to descend steep paths in order to swim. The rocks in the ocean resemble monoliths in their own right, an inspiration for countless painters. Particularly famous are Monet's renditions of the aiguilles de Port-Coton called *Les Pyramides.*

It turns out that Belle Ile, being in clear, open sea with a rocky coast, provides a major breeding spot for gooseneck barnacles. Our rental is in a hamlet just outside of Souzon, a small port where leisure craft mix with small commercial fishing boats. *Crêperies,* fish restaurants, and clothing boutiques line the quay, all painted in pastels with a simple design ubiquitous to the island: outlining the windows and doors in deeper pinks, reds, yellows, and blues. At low tide, the long, narrow basin empties almost completely, and the water reveals rich muck between grounded boats. Here the locals rake and trowel, collecting clams, oysters, snails, and small green crabs. Our arrival in Souzon coincides with the presence of a photo installation, which is scattered on large panels throughout the town. The installation's theme is the daring work of gooseneck barnacle fishermen, who hammer and chisel their harvest loose after descending cliffs or jumping from the side of a boat into the Atlantic waves crashing against the cliffs. The men are clad in rubber boots and suits to protect them from both the cold sea and the sharp rocks, and they wear flotation vests in case they get knocked out or washed away. Special gloves protect their hands against the sharp shells so that they can work vigorously at low tide, the only time they're able to harvest. All in all, gathering gooseneck barnacles is the extreme-sport version of seashore foraging.

Each morning I venture into the town of Le Palais for the market, which consists of one goat farmer selling his cheese, two vegetable stands, one charcuterie, and five fish sellers, two of whom sell only the daily catch from a single boat. The fish they peddle have a special name: *poissons sauvages de petit bateau.* Being wild, they're considered the freshest and healthiest.

I speak to a fish vendor who displays several kilos of gooseneck barnacles.

"Are those local?"

"Of course. Belle Ile is where most of the *pouce-pieds* in France come from," the vendor replies. Could this be true? Wouldn't they get fished out quickly on a small island? Whatever the case, it's clear that I have inadvertently come to France's gooseneck barnacle mines. I buy a half pound of barnacles along with a local pink clam and live *bouquet* shrimp. Our first dinner will be a feast.

I visit the goat cheese vendor, whose farm is only a kilometer from where we are staying. He sells mainly fresh goat cheese with a variety of coatings, including shallots, fines herbes, and pepper. But I am immediately drawn to the *fromage de chèvre frais aux algues.* The cheese is coated with finely chopped flecks of purple dulse and green sea lettuce. Goat cheese and seaweed is not an intuitive combination, so naturally we have to try it.

The gooseneck barnacles are far fresher than the first ones Mary and I tried. In fact, I realize they are living, something that I hadn't been sure of the night of our initiation. I open the claw end to inspect the cirri and am struck by how much they resemble the crest of a cockatoo, in miniature, of course. Though ill-equipped and inexperienced, I still feel the urge to try gathering some myself.

Like all of Brittany, Belle Ile has a *sentier du littoral,* a coastal walking path, a circuit of approximately sixty miles. On mainland Brittany, the coastal path is a thousand miles long. It's known as the *sentier des douaniers,* since for centuries foot patrols policed the shore against the landing of contraband. On Belle Ile, guides organize pleasant four- or five-day walking tours known for their breathtaking views and agreeable bed-and-breakfasts.

I scout passages down the cliffs. Strolling along the *sentier du littoral,* one encounters signs urging walkers to respect the flora restoration project on the moors and beware the mortal dangers of cliff edges. I'm mindful of both—particularly the latter.

I soon discover that wild edibles abound on the island. Sea beet grows at the nearest beach, and large patches of sea purslane gain rootholds even in front of the famous aiguilles de Port-Coton. Nests of rock samphire, once a significant food source for the Celts, thrive on the cliffs. The plant is covered with yellow flowers this time of year. These greens can all be cooked like asparagus, and rock samphire is often pickled and packed in seawater and sold in major cities. Sea beet, sometimes called sea spinach, offers an edible root as does sea holly, that prickly plant that sets barefooted beachgoers dancing. I also find stands of orach, which can also be prepared like spinach.

At times the trail dips into small pockets of trees and greenery, where the air is suffused with the odor of mint and ripe blackberries. Stalks of wild fennel tower in the meadows and along the roadside, just beginning to turn autumn-brittle. Their flowers have a compound umbrella-like stem structure, with smaller stem clusters of yellow flowers that become fennel seeds. Discovering thyme near a wild apple tree, I recall the Old English "Nine Herbs Charm":

> Remember, Mugwort, what you made known,
> What you arranged at the Great proclamation.
> You were called Una, the oldest of herbs,
> you have power against three and against thirty,
> you have power against poison and against infection,
> you have power against the loathsome foe roving
> through the land.

Straying from the trail to one beach to find a discreet bush for Mary, we come upon freshly emerging *rosés de prés,* the common field mushroom of my friend Jean-Pierre's youth. Near them stands a wild pear tree, laden with rock-hard, flavorless fruit. What the hell can we do with these? Nothing, probably.

One of the parts of Belle Ile that is most photographed in storms and on sunny days alike is La Pointe des Poulains because of its panoramic view over the barren rocky peninsula in the open sea. In rough weather spectacular waves crash against the cliffs. A small white lighthouse with a square tower stands romantically isolated against the elements. It operates independently powered by solar panels. Sarah Bernhardt, France's most famous actress, bought a small austere military fort in the area and used it for a retreat, building a compound for family and friends at some distance from her own home.

I soon realize that rabbits have overrun the island, their holes and droppings everywhere on the brink of a golf course. How many golf balls end up in rabbit holes, not to mention the Atlantic Ocean? Hares are the island's largest wild mammal, proliferating without any predators to speak of. Certain locals, after some *apéros* at the bar, report wild boar spottings, but even though boars can swim for many miles, the reports are met with derisive laughter. Along the path, we find places where gulls have regurgitated shells, the vast majority of these coming from gooseneck barnacles. It appears that the gulls, like the Spanish and the Portuguese, are *percebes* connoisseurs.

At 6:00 a.m. the tide is at just the right height. I leave for the coast after walking the dogs on the farm road, scattering alarmed rabbits left and right, and drive up toward Sarah Bernhardt's fortress, which assumes a particularly menacing gothic aura just before daybreak. Stars are still glimmering above, but the ground is draped in a thin mist anywhere the plateau dips. I park the car and take the path to the spot I have selected, a place where the sea churned up at low tide for no good reason—no wind, clear weather, some disturbance offshore, probably. It's light enough for me to make my way down the cliff path, until at a certain point I find myself in difficulty, lacking the confidence to go either up or down. I feel trapped in the rough-sculpted rock above the turbulent sea, the textured formula for a Monet painting. Working to regain composure, I ask myself why on earth I'm doing this. On the verge of breaking my neck, I vow to bring *Ariel's Ghost* next time and set off from the cove below Sarah Bernhardt's austere domain. Perhaps I will bring diving gear, for good measure.

7

A SEAWEED THANKSGIVING

WHILE HENRY JAMES famously observed in a letter that "it's a complex fate, being an American," and James Baldwin struggled to define what being American even means, I rarely mull over questions of national identity, living here in France. It's complicated, however, for an American expatriate to explain the strange phenomenon called Thanksgiving. My mother, in her eighties, is a devotee of American Thanksgiving, though she lives in a remote canal village in Burgundy and is obliged to special-order her whole turkey, an item usually available in France only at Christmas. The rest of the year turkey comes disassembled, mainly in the form of escalopes.

Our French friends are always keen on celebrating a food-oriented fête with us, even when the occasion commemorates the survival of a band of opportunists and religious separatists struggling against the savage rigors of the New World, where (or so they believed) the devil's agents lurked behind every rock and tree to sign up souls. The holiday serves as my mother's excuse to cook a meal so Lucullan that our friends fully experience the American practice of eating one's way to writhing misery. My mother's version of this feast involves not only super-sizing but also putting an army of irresistible foods on the table, something rivaling the meal prepared in *Babette's Feast.*

While my mother loves to experiment with cuisine, she is assiduous about preparing the traditional Thanksgiving fare, particularly when cooking for the French: turkey with cornbread, fruit, and nut dressing; rich gravy; mashed white potatoes with plenty of butter; roasted parsnips; sweet potatoes candied or puréed with sherry; Brussels sprouts with chestnuts; cranberry and orange sauce; baked breads, butter-flake rolls, and biscuits. Some of these dishes are uncommon in France. Our French *invitées* are informed in advance that there will be no entrée or cheese courses, so they must prepare to survive on the main meal. The fatal trap lies in her three pies: apple, pumpkin, and pecan, followed by mini mince and lemon tarts. Our polite guests feel duty-bound to try all offerings, finishing with digestifs.

Thanksgiving is my favorite holiday, though I can't really put my finger on why, beyond the simplicity of the great traditional meal amid late autumn's seasonal shifts of both light and weather. The odors and kitchen warmth as winter approaches have a primal appeal. While we can trace harvest-festival traditions throughout the world—they probably date back to Neolithic times—the American Thanksgiving is heavily colored by its starvation narrative and the encounter between two vastly different worlds. The national holiday that arose from that early incident is founded on an appealing myth of friendship and generosity. Maybe this is why Thanksgiving seems to have taken off in France.

My role in the proceedings, besides playing *sous-chef* and busboy, is to recount for our guests the tale of the first Thanksgiving, a story that grows ever more jumbled and historically occult when one considers the implications of the Mayflower Compact and the fate of the native people. Somehow the story of the Pilgrims overcoming their period of starvation and disease has evolved into a holiday requiring the annual sacrifice of some 40 million turkeys. "The first Thanksgiving" is almost always presented in a condensed popularized myth: Indians saved a wayward band of sick and starving English settlers by teaching them to bury two herring for each mound of soil into which they plant corn, squash, and beans. Following a rich harvest, the Indians and pilgrims celebrated, feasting, sharing games, and praying together for five days. Some of this may be true.

As a kid foraging for food along the New England seashore, I always wondered what the hundred-plus religious "saints" and entrepreneurs could have eaten to stave off starvation and fortify themselves against disease during their brutal winter. Just three months after arriving in November 1620, only half of the original group remained alive, most dying in January and February. Why didn't the Pilgrims just help themselves to snails, cattails, fern roots, clams, and mussels, I wondered? Why didn't they just eat seaweed?

Many years later, my curiosity evolved into a strong desire to go to Plymouth, Massachusetts, for Thanksgiving. Plimoth Plantation is a living museum retaining the seventeenth-century spelling of the seaside town in England for which it was named. A passionate historian, Henry Hornblower II, created Plimoth in 1947, starting with two shacks. Decades on, the museum hosts "America's Thanksgiving Dinner," which in a kind of delusion I imagined included dining with the Wampanoag. I called Plimoth Plantation to reserve a place for one of the three sittings on Thanksgiving Day.

"I'm sorry, sir, 'America's Thanksgiving Dinner' is sold out. But we still have tickets for the 'Thanksgiving Day Buffet' and the 'Courtyard Buffet.'"

"Nothing for 'America's Thanksgiving Dinner'? I live in France, and I'm researching wild edibles. I'd really like to talk to the Wampanoag."

"Excuse me, you want to talk to the Wampanoag?"

"I mean at 'America's Thanksgiving Dinner.'"

A worrying silence followed, but then, "Sir? We found one remaining place for the 6:00 p.m. sitting. Is that acceptable?"

Acceptable? I was delighted. A ticket to "America's Thanksgiving Dinner," including a two-day entry to the Wampanoag Village, the Plantation, and the Mayflower facsimile!

Just a few weeks before my flight, the Northeast was hit by the gargantuan Hurricane Sandy, followed by a fierce nor'easter that, paradoxically, cleared the air for stunning autumnal weather. I love touring the States, and before arriving in Plymouth my plan was to explore the Chesapeake Bay, partly because I was fascinated by the story of Jamestown, the famous settlement on what was once one of the great food-source-rich estuaries in the world. Captain Smith and his colony fared worse than William Bradford's *Mayflower* Pilgrims, suffering the loss of 80 percent of their colonists in 1609–10, their starving time a decade earlier. Archaeological pit finds from those years reveal that the desperation portion of their fare consisted of birds, musk turtles, dogs, rats, and snakes.

Mary's family roots go back to Williamsburg, and she has fond memories of fishing with her Uncle Fred, nicknamed Hihop—a curious appellation for the Episcopalian bishop of Virginia, who had a shore house at

Sandy Point. Decked out in Bermuda shorts, Hihop and ten-year-old Mary would set out in a motorboat from the mouth of the Potomac to fish with peelers, soft-shell crabs that were universal bait. Apparently Hihop was impressed with Mary's tolerance for getting crab guts on her hands and the whole messy business of bait fishing. "We must have caught something worth keeping," she says now. "Uncle Fred taught me to scale."

The Chesapeake Bay has suffered enormous environmental pressures from poor agricultural practices, various forms of pollution, and a huge, ever-increasing local population. Washington, D.C., Baltimore, and Annapolis are all situated on the edges of this vulnerable water system. During World War II, the bay was a torpedo-testing zone, which resulted in major fish kills. In the 1970s, a marine dead zone developed from decaying algae following a nitrogen-fueled algal bloom, a phenomenon that would soon be seen in Long Island Sound and elsewhere. At one time, the oyster population could filter the whole estuary in three days; now, with the devastation of the beds, it would take a year or more. The salt meadows and marshes full of cordgrass, goldenrod, arrowhead, button bush, pickerel weed, rice cutgrass, sweet flag irises, and cattails play a role in absorbing chemicals and toxins and oxygenating the shallows for creatures. The bay is a place where my father goes even now to hunt for fossils and Indian relics on the banks of the tidal rivers, and he gave me tips for my travels.

After two days of scouting the Chesapeake Bay and sampling local oysters, blue crab, and clams, I headed north to Plymouth. Settling in at the Pilgrim Sands, a hotel on the bay with a view of Eel Pond and the Plantation, I took a walk, poking along the shoreline and surveying the sea lettuce, bladder wrack, dulse, kelp, and thongweed. The storms, in addition to hurling sea rocks into parking lots and across roads, had torn loose a good deal of fresh-looking seaweed, although spring is supposed to be the best season for harvesting. I picked some from several different patches, absorbed in the novelty of eating seaweed at the spot where Bradford, Standish, and Brewster once stood and the Pilgrims finally settled.

I wonder whether those long-ago travelers realized that sea lettuce could be used in nutritious soups and salads? It's rich in vitamins, minerals, protein, and fiber, and even contains a few calories, though you'd need to eat nearly a hundred grams of it to get the equivalent of a slice of bread with a tad of butter and jam. Seaweed contains vitamin E, allegedly an invigorator of sperm, though perhaps this was not a particularly high priority at the time.

Seaweed is often considered a diet food. Our baker puts *algue* into a type of bread known as *ligne* (for slimming the lines). Brittany, on the other hand, has a traditional butter concoction, hardly dietetic, called *beurre aux algues,* and the Welsh favor a heart-attack-on-a-plate breakfast item called "laverbread"—a seaweed-oatmeal mixture fried in bacon fat. Still, seaweed's nutritional values are far higher than those of garden lettuce, cabbage, carrots, or the world's healthiest food, broccoli. Dulse has twice the protein value of sea lettuce. Though rubbery like all seaweed, it has a pleasant flavor: iodine, salt, slightly sweet, slightly fishy.

Exploring, I encountered vast colonies of common periwinkles, the same snails sold by every fishmonger in Paris. Almost every rock I turned over unveiled some twenty scurrying green crabs even this late in the season. Neither species arrived in America until the 1800s, however, so no help to the Pilgrims in the form of periwinkle chowder or broiled soft-shell green crabs.

At low tide on Thanksgiving Day, I walked the length of a three-mile spit called Long Beach, one of the most beautiful sand-barrier stretches I know. It provides shelter for the port of Plymouth and now enjoys environmental laws protecting dune grasses and coastal nesting. On the outer shore of Long Beach, the storms had unearthed, or unsanded, enormous sea clams. Just one or two could make a filling soup, or the muscle could be sliced for Thanksgiving sashimi.

Seagulls, true master foragers bold enough to saunter into stores and steal bags of potato chips, had pecked apart razor clams and small crabs, and the clean shell fragments littered the waterline. Gulls know how to dig for hard-shell clams and then drop them from high up on hard surfaces to open them. Crabs are common prey, of course.

I discovered that, after the storms on the inner shore, sand and mud at least three inches deep had shifted, revealing tens of thousands of shells in a vertical position: razor clams, soft-shells, quahogs, all shellfish that had died naturally. I'd never seen anything quite like it. The storm surge had uncovered what we don't ordinarily see in the tidal flats, much of which disintegrates naturally. I found oysters and mussels, and everywhere clams sending up mini *jets d'eau,* little squirts of water. In a half hour, I could have collected enough shellfish to make a *cioppino* for a family, and I saw that others had had the same thought: several locals were digging, admirably keeping up with the gulls. One older man waded in the Eel River with a scoop net.

"What are you netting?" I asked.

"Grass shrimp."

"You eat grass shrimp?" It seemed like a reasonable question, considering that the French eat any kind of shrimp over a half inch long.

"Not if you don't want fluke worms."

"Well, then, what are you doing?"

"Catching bait." I felt a bit stupid. Grass shrimp, like peelers, attract a wide range of fish, including trout, weakfish, hake, and flounder.

With all the wild bounty here, it's hard to understand why so many of the Pilgrims starved. Winter foraging parties managed only to pilfer small Indian stores and steal a deer from wolves. They killed three seals, shot some birds, and caught a codfish. Not exactly enough to feed a colony.

In truth, it's a miracle that anyone survived the *Mayflower* adventure, since they started late and suffered storms and many on board were ill partly due to the unhealthiness of their own provisions. Mid-ocean in foul weather, the mainsail beam cracked, and typical November and December storms forced them on arrival to the New World to backtrack from what is now New York from their destination in Virginia to take refuge in the calmer waters of Massachusetts Bay. The *Mayflower* anchored and parties were sent to scout out a viable site with a defensible hill and rivers and ponds. They found an ideal location, Patuxet, where European disease had already killed off the local Wampanoag group. The disease, still under debate, was so swift and complete that the Pilgrims discovered unburied skeletons.

After Patuxet was discovered, the *Mayflower* sailed across the bay and was forced to anchor more than a mile from the shallow shore. Six healthy pilgrims, including Bradford, Brewster, and Standish, treated the sick, cleaned them, and rowed to land to gather food and build a village center.

In March, the local Wampanoag sachem, Massasoit, sent Samoset to make a peace pact with the Pilgrims. Samoset boldly walked into the English encampment, startling the settlers by speaking their language. He and the Europeans established a peace treaty and agreed to join forces against the powerful Narragansett tribe. Samoset returned the next day with Tisquantum, better known as Squanto, the Wampanoag whose kidnapping took him to Spain as a slave and then later to England. He and Samoset lived with the Pilgrims and taught them the survival skills of planting, fishing, foraging, and preserving. Squanto was considered a "special instrument of God" by Pilgrim leaders and an outright traitor by some tribal members. He died on November 30, 1622, one year after the "First Thanksgiving," from an "Indian fever" that may have been poisoning.

I was enthralled with the Wampanoag village. The Indians spoke to us of bark huts, dugout canoes, the process of tanning deer hide using first the deer's own brain enzymes followed by stretching them over smoke. Scientists, doctors, and naturalists visiting with their families added to the conversation with their own expertise, pointing out blue-stain fungus in a newly hewn canoe or offering professional speculations on the diseases that claimed so many lives before the arrival of the Pilgrims. One of the latest candidates was leptospirosis, contracted by humans through rat urine in fresh water.

At "America's Thanksgiving Dinner," I was seated with a jolly Montana strip miner and his family, and we swapped stories about wild edibles on our respective continents. The Wampanoag, however, were nowhere to be found. I approached the program host, who in his role as Pilgrim leader was clad in tights, billowing pants, and knitted hat.

"Why didn't the Pilgrims eat seaweed if they were starving?"

The faux Pilgrim was courteous, a patient veteran of thousands of dingbat questions. He responded as if we were in the seventeenth century.

"I shan't survive on seaweed, my good feller."

I returned to the strip miner and his kind family, and enjoyed a very good meal in their company.

I flew back to France inspired by my Plimoth Plantation experience. I told Mary of my plans to plant a Wampanoag garden in the spring if I could find herring that were not smoked or pickled. More daringly, I elected to tinker with my mother's near-sacred Thanksgiving menu, an act verging on sedition. I would invent a new dish using seaweed, I decided. I gave eels serious consideration: with the help of Squanto, their fatty, nutritious flesh had become a major staple for the colonist. I wonder what the eel equivalent of 40 million turkeys would be?

One of the very first meals I made as a kid was Rock Cornish game hen with wild rice stuffing. My grandmother, who worked as the hostess at the Red Barn Restaurant, offered me a dinner and a movie for my birthday. I chose Rock Cornish game hen because I thought it really was a game bird; it had to be, didn't it, with wild rice that I just knew the Indians had collected from the edges of lakes? Imagine my disappointment when I learned it was a bird invented for commercial purposes, something like the Portobello mushroom. Still, the idea of wild rice thrilled me.

I also remember making Thanksgiving dinner in the throes of student poverty—the closest a middle-class kid usually comes to "starving time." With the only cash I had, I bought a turkey, stuffed it with a spinach-and-oyster dressing, and roasted it in a wok. I invited two similarly impoverished friends, and the success of my Thanksgiving offering astonished them nearly as much as it did me.

Back to the present day, though: why not try a seaweed dressing? I made one with wakame, dulse, kelp, wild mushrooms, tofu, oysters, ginger, garlic, and spices, and tested it first on a chicken, which I served with an Asian sauce. To be honest, the thought of making a tofurky crossed my mind, since seaweed and tofu often accompany each other. I've had nontraditional Thanksgiving dinners before. One memorable one was in a hunting shack in Mississippi brush lands outside of Starkville. Several families got together and prepared two turkeys: one injected with Cajun spices and the other deep-fried whole in a barrel of oil suspended over a fire. Probably the latter method would not have been approved by the fire department, but the result was delicious. Kids shot off fireworks, lighting up a neighbor's "spirit tree"—bottles hung with string in the branches.

My mother and Mary humored me through my experiments and were, I think, pleasantly surprised by the results. I felt further inspired to experiment with leftovers. I decided to use them to make sushi rolls that included some panko-fried oysters. I also incorporated Asian ingredients with turkey just to see if the flavors were synergistic. They were.

Encouraged, I proposed that Thanksgiving dinner include up to four different seaweeds. We could use fresh seaweed, maybe rice, and other types of seafood—mussels, shrimp, even limpets, lots of spices, a kind of outside-in paella. My mother cringed.

"It sounds absolutely dreadful!"

It didn't, really—at least, not to me. In the end, though, we served my mother's traditional dinner, to everyone's satisfaction. Our French friends went away as stuffed as Americans, having no idea what sorts of strange Thanksgiving concoctions they were spared.

8

WAKAME DIET

DURING THE YEAR-END holidays in France, traditional fare can start with either foie gras or blinis warmed in hot butter with crème fraîche and *saumon fume;* followed by a *chapon farci,* or a leg of lamb with potatoes and drippings, or a *plateau de fruits de mer* with plenty of mayonnaise. Then comes maybe *vacherin,* the cheese version of lava that you must eat with a spoon, all accompanied with champagne and other wines, and finishing with Calvados. The *bûche de Noël* provides a sensation equivalent to the common "cookie coma." You can ring up calories fast while ringing in the New Year.

My mother, a lifelong veteran of cyclical weight gain and dieting, always warns, "It's not so much the calories as it is the portions you consume." My version is that it's not so much the portions I consume as the hours I am willing to spend running to burn off what I cannot resist. Clearly, self-denial is not a particular strength of mine, but spontaneous acts of repentance can be from time to time.

Starting the New Year in the customary post-holiday spirit, I vow austerity in my diet. The question that I posed to the museum guide at Plymouth took on an altered significance. Why *didn't* the Pilgrims just eat seaweed? Well, seaweed, if uncontaminated, is certainly healthy enough, but it doesn't contain enough calories to ward off starvation. In addition, some brown seaweeds contain fucoxanthin, a carotenoid, which purportedly promotes the burning of fat. This might not have been of much help to starving colonists, but it's suddenly attractive to me, even if merely for its potential placebo effect. I'm curious about seaweed cuisine and the challenges it poses, so a seaweed diet also appeals to me as an adventurous alternative to other forms of losing weight.

I'm not good at keeping resolutions of any kind, but especially those made for the New Year. Starting a diet regime in northern Europe in January feels especially punitive. One lives more in night than day, the temperatures hover near freezing, and the Parisians bundle up in nearly uniform black, never without an umbrella to lose somewhere. Every morning, Mary consults the solar charts that come with the latest post office calendar and calculates each minute of light gained. She monitors the Weather Channel closely for any variation in periods of gray skies and intermittent rain. Sometimes, a thrilling extratropical cyclone is predicted, a barometric trench below a thousand millibars, and she will instigate a race to the sea to watch the mountainous waves off the Breton coast, occasionally rewarded by seeing them surge into seaside towns at high tide. She is never in a dieting frame of mind in January; warm food comforts her, even though she readily admits that eating makes you cold, scientifically speaking. While she has no quibble with seaweed in principle, it's just not the food she craves in the dead of winter. Meanwhile, my mother's assessment of seaweed is unequivocal: "It's fishy."

Despite the lack of enthusiasm around me, I decide that I will eat seaweed, in one form or another, in every meal for a week to see if truly it is a diet food. My experiment will be a solitary one, although friends and family generously share their opinions, most of which convey their doubts about my judgment. One friend warns me against buying seaweed from Japan, reminding me that hundreds of tons of radioactive groundwater are flowing through Fukushima Daiichi into the Pacific. You can see video demonstrations of Geiger counters revving roentgen and sievert clicks over packages of dried wakame and sheets of nori.

Perhaps seaweed from the Irish or Tasmanian coast is safer. However, seaweed farming has existed in Japan since the seventeenth century, starting in Tokyo Bay, and has developed into an important industry in many parts of the world. Brown kelp alone makes up 10 percent of the Japanese diet. Kombu and sheets of nori can be ground up and used as a kind of salt to enhance soups, rice, omelets, and sauces. Nori sheets also possess the novelty factor of being like paper. I make a list of paper foods besides nori sheets: wanton wrappers, Vietnamese rice paper rolls, Greek filo, similar Tunisian brick, and even lasagna, all potentially useful for seaweed dishes. Well, maybe not lasagna, but I'm ruling nothing out.

Except as a condiment in Brittany or a flavorless emulsifier, consumption of seaweed in France is a relatively recent phenomenon. Many have warmed to it as a health food now, whereas previously it was used primarily in hand and face creams, shampoo, and cosmetics. In the last twenty years, Paris has experienced an explosion in the number of Japanese restaurants—there are five within two blocks of my flat—and seaweed salad has become especially popular. Local bio markets sell spirulina in capsule form, the manufacturers boldly claiming that the blue-green *algue* can fortify your body against arthritis, allergies, stroke, hypertension, and Parkinson's disease.

When the time finally arrives for me to plan the week's seaweed meals, the first thing that comes to mind is to explore various avenues for cheating. I decide that while seaweed must constitute a significant part of each meal, it needn't be the principal ingredient. If seaweed provides 10 percent of the Japanese diet, though, then my seaweed diet should aspire to at least double or triple this minimum. My amendment also opens the door for other means of potential fudging or self-trickery; for example, extracts of alginic acid from kelp, carrageenans from Irish moss, and agar from an array of red seaweeds all serve as food additives, mainly for their emulsifying or gelatin-producing qualities, useful in certain German beers, Japanese bean jelly, and American chocolate milk. But while ready to cheat, I'm also eager to experiment seriously.

The second consideration is how to acquire seaweed when Étretat on the Normandy coast, where there's a chance to harvest healthy fresh seaweeds, is at least a two-hour drive from Paris. Like most urban wannabe-epicureans with an interest in seaweed, I simply go to the closest Asian market and buy dried wakame, nori, or kombu. Then I check out the nice variety of dried "sea vegetables," as seaweeds are sometimes called, at the health-food shop on our own street. The true revelation comes when I discover that the fish section of the Bon Marché Grand Epicerie sells containers with *algues sauvages* from Brittany packed in seawater. How unlikely, but wonderful, to have real thongweed, dulse, sea lettuce, and laver readily available just around the corner from us! Granted I'd miss out on the pleasure of collecting them—scrambling over the slippery shore rocks to choose the best purple, olive, brown, and green specimens. The convenience, though, is worth it in the raw weather of midwinter. I start the

Me with sea lettuce and thongweed
(Anse du Guesclin, Brittany)

year testing and inventing cuisine with the materials at hand and come up with fourteen seaweed meals.

As I break the seals on the plastic containers and nibble on the four different seaweeds to get a sense of their texture and flavor, I wonder why no one told me when I was a child forager that most seaweeds are edible. Probably someone taught me when I was poking around through seaweed in tidal ponds that it's not a plant. I've been diving my whole life, sometimes pausing for minutes, mesmerized by the movements of dragon tongues, long flat tails, buoyant fingers, swinging hair, sparkling pink clusters, and green antlers.

Much literature on various seaweeds refers to them as plants, even though the authors concede in the end that seaweed is algae: single-cell organisms living together as an integrated colony. Seaweed grows in littoral zones and at depths in which enough light penetrates for photosynthesis to occur. While appearances might be deceiving, seaweed doesn't have roots but rather attaches itself to various marine substrates, mainly rock. The attaching structures evolved accordingly, often in the form of pods or filaments for hard surfaces or fingerlike haptera for anchoring to the shifting sea bottom in deeper zones. The point is that seaweeds do not absorb water through roots, nor do they distribute sugars produced by photosynthesis through vein structures. Indeed, there is no mechanism to provide nutrition to the entire organism. Each cell in algae supports itself through its own ability to synthesize sugars using pigment and light. As collective organisms, seaweeds possess different features besides holdfasts, including flotation bladders, stems called stipes, and blades. They reproduce sexually or through motile zoospores that find places to attach themselves and sprout a new organism.

I launch my week of seaweed dieting with a conceit: paying homage to Tisquantum and his eels. Eel is not a novelty for me. My father with his primitive pole spear caught eels for the family, and I've tried *fokhagymás-paprikás angolna,* a garlicky Hungarian soup with eel and paprika; Italian *spiedini di anguilla,* eels grilled on skewers, a Sunday family treat; and *gerookte paling,* a revered Dutch smoked-eel sandwich, something on the order of a lobster roll. But my favorite continues to be barbecued *unagi,* Japanese freshwater eel that pairs perfectly with laver, or nori. I often order *unagi chirashi sushi* at restaurants, so I consider making my own version with seaweed by adding it to the bowl of sweetened vinegar-flavored rice and using seasoned wakame with the barbecued eel itself. Instead, though, I settle on a dragon sushi roll since I was born in a dragon year and, more significantly, I've never made one before.

Buying prebarbecued frozen eel from the Asian market is the easiest. The dragon roll by definition requires nori and provides opportunities to work with other seaweeds for decoration, so I am keen to take up the challenge, although it seem a bit extravagant for a lone diner. Dragon rolls, in the hands of a professional sushi chef, can become ingenious food art: pink octopus suckers with red salmon caviar to make dragon eyes; bright red barbecue sauce for fiery wings; shrimp antennae for whiskers; nori sheets cut into shapes; fruits, colored roes, cucumbers, pickled ginger, and avocado all contributing to the effect. Making a dragon is like playing with your food before devouring it.

Since I am just amusing myself anyway, I think, why not make my own nori sheets? On reading about nori workshops, I see that the process basically involves making green edible paper—starting with red algae. Not knowing what it was, I had seen and tasted North Atlantic laver, *Porphyra umbilicali,* as it dried at low tide and rehydrated with the incoming sea. It's a close cousin to what the Japanese use, *Porpyra yezoensis,* so I pulverize some, make the required slurry in a square mold, and press it with a cutting board weighed with a teetering food processor. Paris in misty January isn't ideal for putting drying racks of nori in the sun—I cheat with a hair dryer. I make several sheets in order to have both the purists' raw-foods version and the *yaki nori* roasted version. My nearly black nori works wonderfully for the dragon, giving it a slightly rougher appearance for its dark scales, and makes a more flavorful meal than with factory nori sheets.

I wonder whether any seaweed-based alcohol drinks exist to accompany my dragon roll, but realize quickly that the high salt content and the lack of carbohydrates would not please otherwise-eager yeast cultures. I naïvely blunder into the Japanese ideas of serving sake and food on human bodies: *wakamezake,* a sake tidal pool between the thighs of a woman, pubic hair being seaweed—wakame. This activity goes along with the more established serving idea *Nyotaimori,* literally serving sushi and sashimi on a completely still male or female model's naked body. Food reporters have compared the *Nyotaimori* experience to eating in a morgue, but I can easily imagine how quickly the corpse comes to life with a poorly aimed chopstick pinch.

Mary admires my fiery eel-dragon and enjoys a piece. But for the most part, the two of us part culinary ways for a whole week, despite my attempts to persuade her to join me. "Listen to this. More people in Okinawa than almost anywhere live to over a hundred. Some scientists attribute their longevity to the fucoidan content in their diet from seaweed."

"It's their genes," Mary responds, on her way to make her own dinner.

"It's a sulfated polysaccharide. That sounds healthy, doesn't it?"

"It's just a complex sugar."

Is it the slippery, or should I say slimy, quality of some seaweed dishes that discourages Mary? One thing is clear, a heavy breakfast of seaweed-laden Welsh laverbread is not in her plans no matter how comforting it may be. She is not much of a breakfast person, so I didn't really expect her to share my enthusiasm for the stuff. Since I am working with nori anyway, though, laverbread seems like an obvious choice. The basis of *bara lawr* is nori, or laver, rolled in oats and fried. After reading Robbie Freeman's *First Catch Your Peacock,* I had to try it. His struggle to make it sound appetizing was touching: "Then I came across one of the suggestions for making laverbread: mixed with a few drops of olive oil and lemon juice and pepper, eaten with fingers of dry toast. The similarity with caviare struck me, the alliteration appealed, immediately dubbed it 'Caviare Cymrieg.' Success with laverbread at last—but it was disastrous, really, over the years the name 'Welsh Caviare' has stuck and even been attributed to Richard Burton." The traditional laverbread breakfast with thick bacon fat and fried eggs, which is what I prepare, is not at all as bad as Freeman suggested. Laverbread, touted for its oyster flavor, is milder than I was expecting and synergetic, as many foods are, with bacon and eggs. American "Hangtown Fry" made up with eggs, bacon, and fried oysters might also garner the attention of heart associations.

Laverbread is traditionally served with cockles as well or in a more fluid form as a kind of sauce on fish, but I save cockles for my next dish, a seaweed risotto, in which I use seaweed in the broth and fold diced thongweed into the rice, along with aged pecorino. The topping combines sautéed cockles, dulse, some bacon bits, and chives (onion grass if it were spring). From this dish, I learn that thongweed, which the French call both *spaghetti de mer* and *haricots de mer,* is especially easy to use in cuisine because of its *sous-le-dent* slightly crunchy texture and delicate sweet salt flavor. I quickly run out of thongweed as it becomes a favorite among the seaweeds, forcing me back to the Bon Marché Grand Epicerie.

In tribute to the lone codfish the Pilgrims caught during their perilous first winter, I prepare a cod dinner with a Breton condiment, *tartare aux algues,* in which I include four types of seaweed. Unfortunately for them, the colonists had no garlic, olive oil, lemon, and shallots, although I have no doubt they were grateful for the fish anyway. So many recipes require a catalyst, and for seaweed tartare I discover that mushrooms give the flavor more depth. I add some of the wild mushrooms I gathered last autumn and keep frozen. To add a little Mexican spark I mince a jalapeño pepper and fold that in as well. And, okay, I know that spicy *panko*-fried cod is not exactly dietetic, but instinct tells me that it will be synergetic with tartare.

Cockle, mushroom, and seaweed soup (Paris)

Returning to Asian dishes, I make a classic wakame salad, but to mitigate the wimp factor I include jellyfish, which to my surprise is crunchy and great with the sauce. Whether you become a fan of jellyfish or not, there's always the noble consolation of eating invasive species, or plaguing creatures associated with global warming. I often find that one idea for a meal begets the next, partly through the desire for a new experience and partly because I have leftover ingredients. The latter is the case with the soup I make next. I use sea lettuce, cockles, black cod, and two types of mushrooms in a delicate vegetable broth, creating one of my most successful dishes. Mary consents to eat a small bowlful and loves it. She is further charmed by imperial rolls—a paper food consisting of seaweed, shrimp, and wild mushrooms wrapped in lettuce and mint. I add the common Vietnamese fish sauce *nuoc-mâm* and some scrapings of ginger and carrots. For Vietnamese rice paper seaweed wraps, I simply stir-fry sea lettuce, tofu, mushrooms with garlic, ginger, sesame oil, soy sauce; add a line of hoisin on dampened rice paper; roll with herbs; and eat with a dipping sauce.

Switching back to European-style cuisine, I make seaweed *tapenade,* an intense seaweed condiment that includes some anchovies, which I use in a whelk starter and pollock main course. After a few other inspiring dishes, I finish with seaweed mayonnaise for avocado and *bouquet,* a true *pêche-à-pied* shrimp often sold alive in fish markets. *Bouquet* are highly esteemed, delicate-flavored shrimp that are sometimes eaten alive, something I thought was only done in the Thai "dancing shrimp" dish and the Scandinavian fjord shrimp on ice and brown butter. I try live shrimp despite my recent discovery that grass shrimp can carry fluke worms. I argue to myself that they are alive and beautiful, translucent like the open waters that they come from.

In the end, my personal theory that the Pilgrims might have eaten seaweed to survive was in effect proven wrong. The line of the Pilgrim reenactor from "America's Thanksgiving Dinner" keeps echoing in my thoughts: "I shan't survive on seaweed, my good feller." I don't know why, but I did lose weight, five pounds in a week, while eating some very high-calorie foods. One might think that a sushi dragon isn't caloric, but eight pieces comes in at just under 600 calories, and that also greatly depends on how monstrous you fancy your dragon to be. Who could estimate the calories in a laverbread breakfast, a risotto with some cheese and bacon, fried cod with seaweed tartare, or fried seaweed imperial rolls?

In the wild, seaweed has its own powerful allure—stunning autumnal colors, dramatic shapes, and hypnotic movements suggesting tongues, wings, or ghosts. Kelp forms forests, which have their own mysterious darkness. As with mushrooms, one should follow rules when foraging. Collect the plants with scissors, take only a portion, leave enough for the algae to live on, and avoid collecting everything from a single place.

When I mentioned to my doctor that most seaweeds on the rocks were edible, he took it to heart. The next time he visited his home in Brittany, where seaweed heaps on the rocks at low tide, he walked the shoreline, sampling this plant and that as I'd suggested. Maybe this is what Anne Morrow Lindbergh meant when she wrote: "The sea does not reward those who are too anxious, too greedy, or too impatient. To dig for treasures shows not only impatience and greed, but lack of faith. Patience, patience, patience, is what the sea teaches. Patience and faith. One should lie empty, open, choiceless as a beach—waiting for a gift from the sea." I like the sound of that: to have patience and faith; to lie empty waiting for a gift. Just in case, though—being a hypochondriac—I ordered Spirulina from an Internet pharmacy.

9

GREENS CRAZY

MY MOTHER REPORTS that as a toddler I ate fistfuls of grass, undoubtedly because in the spring sun, or newly cut in the rain, it smells heavenly. For Wordsworth, this irresistible odor was imbued with the "glory and freshness of a dream," wistful longings for intimations of youthful oneness with nature. Byron wrote that "all things that have been born were born to die, / And flesh which Death mows down to hay is grass; / You've pass'd your youth not so unpleasantly." And Shelley observed that the "sound of vernal showers / On the twinkling grass, / Rain-awakened flowers." In unpoetic reality, however, the fragrance of grass is the result of trauma: injured grass emits its own version of an SOS distress call in the form of GLVs—green leaf volatiles. As most of us know, lawns are not particularly digestible for humans, although even the Vicomte de Mauduit in his wartime book *You Can't Ration These* recalls J. R. B. Branson's rhapsody, "Eating beautiful fresh green grass, and beautiful fruit, and the petals of beautiful flowers, are merely incentives that I suggest towards the expression of that ego in terms of beauty, of delicacy, of refinement" and concedes, "I am no faddist; but always willing to also experience myself the teachings of others."

I admit to buying a can of Chinese grass jelly and finding it underwhelming. The truth is that as lovely as grasses are, with their vaunted spiritual and aesthetic properties, many of the weeds that invade them are much more nutritious. These plants have their own vernal perfumes and spring's dizzy intimations of eternal youth.

On a whim one March, Mary and I drove through the Swiss Alps and the Ligurian Apennines to spend a week on the Riviera di Levante.

"I'm so sick of gray and dark," Mary complained. "I need some sun!"

To me, a friend had suggested, "You are in search of the legacy of poets."

Golfo dei Poeti—the Gulf of Poets—is where Shelley took up residence and Byron dazzled locals with his swimming prowess. The unfortunate Shelley, a reckless skipper and poor swimmer, lost his life sailing into a squall near Viareggio and was cremated on the beach. One comes to Liguria to worship the sea.

"No," I replied, "I'm going for the weeds."

And I was, too, because no one is more weed-crazy than the Italians. Still, I insisted on bringing my boat. After all, didn't I name it *Ariel's Ghost* after Shelley's ill-fated craft?

Mary laughed incredulously when I told her my plan.

"In winter? Shelley died in July, for God's sake."

We packed my boat and electric motor anyway, her cello and sheet music, all our kitchen supplies, and three dogs. This is what spontaneity has come to: an encumbering multiplicity of needs.

I had been reading studies of Italian communities where gathering and cooking weeds remains in practice, despite the general erosion of "traditional knowledge" due to socioeconomic shifts that have marooned old folks in decaying rural villages. The slow-food movement has resurrected cuisine using dandelions, daisies, chicory, onion grass, plantago, mustard, purslane, mint, fennel, and who knows what else. Studies cite *Borago officinalis* as the weed most commonly collected in Italy, with wild asparagus coming in second. *Borago officinalis* is the gorgeous starflower, or borage, a common potherb seemingly known to everyone but me. It turns out that nearly every *pasta fresca* shop in the region of Liguria features *ravioli di borragine.* Being a relative neophyte in the gathering of edible weeds, I made borage my prime target—among other reasons, for its sheer beauty.

In our capricious pursuit of sun and weeds, Mary and I managed to slip through the beginnings of a nasty, late-season blizzard via the Great Saint Bernard Tunnel, but arrived in the town of Sestri Levante in a full-blown tempest, the raging surf and gale conjuring visions of poor Shelley's fate. I admit I questioned my own judgment in bringing the boat. We chose the seaside town between Genoa and Cinque Terre admittedly for nostalgic reasons. In our younger days, we had swum in the Bay of Silence in the morning, and late in the evening promenaded Via Vittorio Veneto along the beaches on the Bay of Fairy Tales. It was packed with generations of Italian families, children on a manic ice-cream high from the *gelaterie.*

The name Bay of Fairy Tales comes from Hans Christian Andersen's short sojourn writing in the area.

We found a dog-friendly apartment rental in an elaborately terraced villa next to the Santo Stefano del Ponte church. The apartment came with a microscopic but well-equipped kitchen for our weed-based culinary experiments.

Even off-season, Liguria offers rugged beauty and an exceptional range of vegetation. This is where the Alps reach the Mediterranean coast: palm trees and macchia shrublands meet olive, orange, lemon, avocado, and pine trees. Each town, it seems, is situated in a cupped bay where small mountain rivers flow into the sea. Amid buildings painted ochre, lime, and warm rust, trompe l'oeil makes an occasional appearance, lending an air of playfulness.

Locating a market was the first order of business, and we soon found ourselves passing grim vendors with rained-soaked shirts and dresses flapping in the wind. Two vegetable stands were dedicated exclusively to greens, and boasted crates of chicory, broccoli rabe, turnip tops, kale, beet greens, chard, cress, and small artichokes on stalks. Even our highly touted Paris *biomarché,* where a Dixie cup full of grass juice costs seven dollars, couldn't come close to matching the array. One section was devoted to *prebuggiun,* a local term that may be loosely translated as "a mess of stuff." I pointed to the sign, lifted my eyebrows, and shrugged my shoulders in what I hoped was universal sign language for "What in the world is it?" The vendor nodded in understanding and started packing plastic bags with different greens, including *scorzonera* tops, *ortica* (nettles), *tarassaco o dente di leone* (dandelions), and, to my delight, *borragine* (borage). He talked in Italian while in mime chopping the "mess" of greens with an imaginary knife and throwing them into an invisible pot. Meanwhile Mary picked out Italian words like *bollire,* which she interpreted as "boil until done."

Before we could leave, the vendor pointed adamantly at a grasslike vegetable labeled with magic marker on cardboard as *agretti.* Both the TV cooking guru Jamie Oliver and the author Frances Mayes wax poetic about *agretti,* describing it as the very essence of spring. Its botanical name is *Salsola soda,* and it's also known as *roscano,* friar's beard, saltwort, *barilla,* or Russian thistlewort. A true wild edible, *agretti* grows in the Mediterranean marshes and is a succulent closely related to samphire, which I have collected in Brittany and Arcachon. The "sal" in the name *Salsola* means "salt." Historically, *agretti* was used to desalinate soil and also provided soda ash for Venetian glassmaking.

I tasted a stem of this "marsh grass" and instantly understood its allure—the fresh spring crunch, the hint of bitterness and salt. Mary held up two fingers, asking *quanto tempo* for boiling friar's beard, and the vendor held up five. We walked back to the car, crunching on strands and leaves of Mediterranean weeds.

The secret to cooking greens the Italian way is quite simple: after boiling, squeeze the water out and then sauté in a frying pan with garlic and local olive oil, known in Sestri Levante as "Ligurian gold." This minimalist formula applies to cooking most edible weeds, just picked, sometimes almost black, fuzzy at times, and by turns bitter, sweet, and even slightly salty. According to natural food gurus, Italian weeds possess antioxidant powers, and a steady diet of wild greens helps to fight depression; who knows, consuming them might have combated the "romantic melancholy" of those tragic English poets who graced Italy in the early nineteenth century. In any case, artisanal Ligurian gold and weeds form the quintessential slow-food marriage.

Due to Liguria's orographic lift—the upward movement of an air mass as it moves over rising terrain—strong winds and heavy rainfall are common in the region. However, storms come and go quickly, and to Mary's delight the clouds broke even as snow flurries swirled at higher elevations and sunbeams turned the sea light jade through passing skirts of rain. Parts of Liguria remain truly wild, protected by the difficulties posed by steep, often craggy slopes. On my rustic foraging walks with our dogs, Snowbell, a fluffy white Maltese, strutted importantly along, tugging at a black leash that bore the legend "Wild Forever" in gold lettering. Many busy locals were cultivating and picking greens from their winter gardens. The others I saw gathering wildflowers and herbs. Wild edibles abounded where the roads died out above the terraced olive groves. Locals would have rolled their eyes at my excitement while collecting various greens and what I thought was borage.

"Foreigners," I imagined them thinking. "So easily pleased!"

I compared the young borage leaves I gathered to those I had bought, and they appeared identical, though Mary eyed them with deep suspicion. The Prime Directive of foraging is, after all, never to eat what you are not absolutely sure of.

To our mutual surprise, we discovered that we needed to take only two steps out of our door to find hedges of wild asparagus bristling with fresh sprouts. Eagerly we began harvesting the spindly stems from our landlord's terrace, and later, on my walks, I collected many more from the boar-ravaged park behind the church of Santo Stefano del Ponte. My progress was slowed only a little by Snowbell, who, despite her "Wild Forever" leash, habitually became ensnared in blackberry brambles.

Finding *Asparagus acutifolius* alone officially confirmed our weed excursion as a triumph against industrial food. Still, since wild asparagus verges on being an ornamental plant in Liguria, even Euell Gibbons of *Stalking the Wild Asparagus* fame would hardly have been impressed. Adventure still called us to the collection of borage and other weeds. For this, we drove into the mountains to Parco Naturale Regionale dell'Aveto, a spectacularly unspoiled part of Italy. I had even read in the local paper that a wolf or a pack of wolves, unafraid of people, was attacking goats up in the hills. While reduced to mere hundreds, wolves were never fully eradicated in Italy, and they are now protected as an endangered species, causing the familiar problems of natural space versus urbanized areas. Farmers kill wolves in protest, and some wolf poachers collect their teeth. Goats pasture, as if free range, on the high slopes. Of several goats mauled by wolves, one was named Heidi and another Snoopy, making me wonder what Italian farmer would come up with names like that.

Once we reached the natural park, Mary, the dogs, and I picked our way carefully along a precipice overhanging a ravine, and I saw for the first time the diaphanous blue of starflowers, each edible blossom with five pointy petals. Once you see the fine hairs, and that color under the curve of the stems, you never forget the flower's soft, blurry look. We began to see starflowers everywhere in impressionistic patches of blue, and we collected plenty of them, along with other weeds for our experiments. These would include our own version of *ravioli di borragine.* Having brought or previously acquired shallots, nutmeg, and Parmesan, we shopped only for good ricotta before returning to our apartment in the villa, where we made a silken pasta dough. This we rolled out as thin as possible and

Nettles and borage used here as topping for oysters (Burgundy)

folded over walnut-sized dollops of borage and ricotta filling, cutting the ravioli rounds with a glass and pinching the edges. Slipped into boiling water, the ravioli cooked relatively quickly. We tossed them in a bowl with butter and Parmesan gratings, and sprinkled delicate blue starflowers over the top. Lovely.

Cooked greens may invite comparisons with spinach, or asparagus, or cucumbers, or grass, but each possesses its own unique flavor and odor, and these sensations unite with a greater overall sense of place. This is the case with borage, but even more so with *Salsola soda.*

"Why don't we substitute *agretti* for pasta and cook up a sort of green capellini?" Mary proposed. "It'd be great with those fiery-looking shrimp."

We knew where to buy *gamberi rossi del Mediterraneo,* still alive at 4:00 p.m. when the boats return to the fishing cooperative in Santa Margherita Ligure, one of a series of coastal resort towns less than twenty miles from Sestri Levante. Between the towns of Chiavari, Zoagli, and Rapallo, the road winds high above the Mediterranean, offering stunning views of the sea and its ever-changing colors.

In Santa Margherita Ligure, fishing boats work through the winter, and since they were enjoying a day of long-awaited calm, the fleet had gone out in full force. However, what started as a nothing-better-than-fresh-off-the-boat expedition for Mary and me left us slightly aghast. The co-op resembled what might have been a vegan's vision of hell, with octopuses making a slithering run for it, eels snaking across the floor, and crates filled with living rays whose tails had been chopped off. Formidable mantis shrimp strong enough to smash glass with their compact claws had been reduced to a seething pile. Amid the chaos, we found a vendor with a dolly loaded with crimson shrimp, and we managed to communicate that we wanted a pound ("*mezzo kilo*") of them.

Walking back along the harbor in Santa Margherita with Mary, I noticed limpets everywhere on the rocks. The breeze had shifted and begun to blow offshore, so the surface of the bay was glassy. I got the idea of taking our boat to a spot away from the harbor to collect limpets. Mary surprised me by agreeing, and the two of us eagerly pumped up the boat in less than ten minutes. We deserted the two smaller dogs in the car for a half hour or so while the Cavalier King Charles manned the prow. *Ariel's Ghost* slipped so naturally over the calm bay it seemed made for these waters, which—sometimes referred to as the Costa dei Delfini—are part of a large dolphin and whale preserve that extends to Sardinia. We had a panoramic view of the majestic hotels: the Imperial Palace, the Hotel Continental, the Metropole, and the Hotel Helios. Churches, villas, and palaces are strewn across precipices, surrounded by citrus trees, umbrella pines, and blue Italian cypresses. I've always enjoyed dreaming myself into places, and at that moment I imagined Liguria, with its dog-crazy people and clear Mediterranean bays beneath towering mountains, as a magical refuge for us in our twilight years. I said as much to Mary, who caught only the phrase "twilight years." She wasn't amused.

"Do you really *have* to be so morbid?"

The farther out we got, the better we could see the snow-capped mountains, which almost seemed to be levitating. We pulled up to a shallow and rocky point. Because the Mediterranean tides are minimal, *pêche à pied* requires hopping right into the water to collect gastropods and mollusks, and that's what I did. Being accustomed to chilly northern ocean water, I was able to wade just long enough to chip off three dozen limpets, smaller than the ones that abound in Brittany, with a large, pointy Sardinian knife.

In a fanciful moment I imagined my ghostly child-self standing on the rocky point, watching critically as I went about my scavenging efforts. Every once in a while it occurs to me that one changes surprisingly little in a lifetime.

Mary stabilized the boat as I hauled myself back into it. The quiet motor powered us back to the boat ramp where we had left the car and miffed dogs, the big deserted hotels shuttered up, the lights of homes and olive farms sprinkled only so far up the slopes.

Back at the apartment, two experiments at once—limpets and red shrimp, both with *agretti.* I cut the body of each limpet from its shell and sliced the foot away from the internal organs and the tiny head. I quickly sautéed them in Ligurian gold with salt and pepper just to see what they tasted like. Mary didn't hesitate to join me in consuming the limpet dish, which we both declared a success, though a bit chewy, as calamari can be. Granted, almost anything sautéed in top-notch olive oil seasoned with salt and pepper has a fair chance of achieving excellence. We were struck not only by how fresh and delicate the dish was but also how stimulating visually, like a plateful of grass with limpets in the form of coins and the freshest, nearly crimson shrimp.

Italy has irresistible traditional dishes that can be readily customized to suit forage foods: pasta, risotto, pizza crust, and crostini. Perhaps the Ligurian offering most likely to corrupt any purist is *foccacia Genovese.* Most people think they know what foccacia is, and no doubt many would argue with me, but no version I've experienced approached the crisp Ligurian variety, with its miniature pools of olive oil. It has been said that foccacia is the sacred ancient flatbread that has stood for the body of Christ. I didn't tell Mary this, because she has a gift for taking something sacred and elevating it to true caloric evil. She immediately put the foccacia in a frying pan, blanketed it with sliced buffalo mozzarella and prosciutto, and, after frying it covered for a few minutes, served it topped with a nest of Italian wild greens. I realized that we could put practically any wild-edible topping on *foccacia Genovese,* and sooner or later we did leftover *gamberi rossi,* a saffron-mussel dish I concocted, and even sautéed *agretti*—essentially, grass on toast.

Wild asparagus grows in southern France but occurs much more sparsely in the north where we live, which seems odd to me since we are not far from the Loire Valley, where cultivated asparagus abounds. Our

Sautéed limpets on rice (Paris)

soil, however, is heavy clay, and asparagus likes sandy, even rocky soil and excellent drainage. This became very plain to me during our holiday. When I headed up the path away from the apartment and used my Sardinian knife to dig up some wild asparagus to take home with me, I found I had to contend with a great many stones all around the roots. Digging up the plants was neither easy nor pleasant.

I also combed the ground below the umbrella pines in the parks to gather seeds. Umbrella pines, also known as stone pine, produce the world's best pine nuts, and one learns quickly why pine nuts are so expensive. Their shells are as hard as pebbles.

Before leaving Liguria, we stopped at a garden store, and I bought some seeds for growing Italian plants—including *agretti* and borage—in our French *potager*. I am well aware that cultivating weeds is far from foraging for wild edibles in Ligurian meadows with our dogs, but we do our best to live "wild forever" no matter what it takes. Shelley's "Ode to the West Wind" came to mind:

> The wingèd seeds, where they lie cold and low,
> Each like a corpse within its grave, until
> Thine azure sister of the Spring shall blow.

Our suffering extremes of weather on the verge of spring made the poem even more relevant. We may have arrived in tempest, but we left

Liguria at 6:00 a.m. in a deluge, the sort that causes road-erasing mudslides. The famed Mussolini work program tunnels, which ordinarily we curse, became our intermittent refuge, although we were forced to squeeze far left because the current of water passing in the slow lane was too deep. Even the villa owner in Sestri Levante called, worried for our safety. The tunnels alternate with breathtaking viaducts, but we couldn't see a thing beyond the steady glow of the taillights of the truck in front of us. Having learned of Liguria's orographic lift, I reasoned that once we turned north and crossed the cloud-trapping Apennines we'd surely escape the torrent. Ultimately my hunch proved right, but not before we endured a number of adrenalin-packed moments hitting pools of water while driving blind.

10

FAMINE-FOOD CULT

RECENTLY A SOUTH AFRICAN preacher named Lesego Daniel commanded his congregation to eat grass in order to feel closer to God. Humans, he claimed, "can eat anything to feed their bodies and survive on whatever they choose to eat." While most of us would not graze on our lawns unless starving, the family of grasses—which includes wheat, rice, corn, and bamboo—represents the world's greatest human food source, proving we are more graminivorous than we might suspect. "One thing people probably don't realize is that humans are basically grass eaters," observed the geochemist Benjamin H. Passey. "We eat grass in the form of the grains we use to make breads, noodles, cereals and beers, and we eat the animals that eat the grass."

Nevertheless, demonstrating that you can eat anything to sustain your body can be tricky business, and an unfortunate mistake might convey you closer to God faster than you had bargained for. Growing up in humid subtropical New Orleans, Mary and her older sister liked to pretend that they were Paleolithic hunter-gatherers—or, as they would have said, "cave-kids"—and on one occasion collected and ate the elephant ears that grew in their yard. While some elephant-ear species provide an important staple in Southeast Asia, Hawaii, India, and Africa, those of the garden variety, specifically caladium, contain a high concentration of oxalic acid, the stuff used to remove calcium from your coffee machine. Plenty of the most common vegetables, cultivated and wild, contain oxalic acid, sometimes providing an agreeable sour taste, as in sorrel, but when more concentrated, as in elephant ears, it burns the tongue and causes vomiting, a painful lesson in the hidden perils of a paleo diet. Oxalic acid crystals can contribute to kidney stones, something from which Mary occasionally suffers, though probably not because of her elephant-ear-eating days.

My childhood weed experiences were far more pedestrian. I collected dandelion greens, or *pissenlit*—French vernacular for "piss in bed," referring to the plant's diuretic powers. The common name comes also from the French, *dent-de-lion,* or lion's tooth, slurred into dandelion. My mother used to drop my brother and me off with our sitter, Mrs. Hayes, a sturdy, unflappable farm woman with her own covey of kids. An enormous stove squatted in the kitchen entryway, and a kettle fizzing oil for frying doughnuts often sat on the stove. Mrs. Hayes bribed us with doughnuts to collect dandelion greens. A mess of kids deployed in the dairy-farm pasture and returned with heaps of dandelion greens within ten minutes, despite some of us in our overzealousness getting our brains zapped out bending over electric fences. Mrs. Hayes's preparation was simple: she just washed the greens and sautéed them—bits of grass, no doubt, and all—in a pot with butter or bacon.

The reviled dandelion is in fact a remarkable plant: the rosette structure of toothy leaves with arrowhead-like tips designed to funnel rainwater to the large taproot; the nastic closure of its sunny flower with the onset of darkness; and its dispersion system, in which each seed drifts off on a delicate starlike plume of fine hairs (pappus), parachuting sometimes miles away. Dandelions have figured prominently in the Eurasian diet since prehistory and are increasingly found in markets both in Europe and the United States.

While nearly every garden store in France sells seeds for *pissenlit,* perfect-lawn people in North America grumble at the colonists for introducing it. It would not be surprising if the Pilgrims had brought dandelion seeds with them, considering the period's general belief that the leaves, roots, and blossoms provide a tonic effect, particularly for stomach, liver, and skin ailments.

These days children often are taught a little elementary botany at summer camp—in the field, you might say—and some are even tutored in Geographical Information Systems and Aerial Sensor Technology, both useful for farming and forestry. I recently visited a natural history museum in Raleigh, North Carolina, where kids were not permitted to enter certain exhibitions without a guide, or without receiving an hour-long lesson in forms of laboratory analysis. Not being a child myself, I was asked outright what I was doing there, and where my guide was.

Back in the days when I actually *was* a child, and to my deep chagrin now, my brother and I behaved very condescendingly in our Trail Master courses in summer day camp and our marine-biology-poking-around-in-tide-pool classes. Digging up sassafras was second nature to us, and we were well aware that the roots were useful for natural, Paugussett-style dental hygiene. We relished the root-beer flavor as much as did the Europeans, whose enthusiasm for the taste made sassafras one of the most prized colonial exports. Little did anyone suspect that the safrole in sassafras would come to be considered poison, which is to say, carcinogenic. The ill effects defy logic, given that every beast in the forest seems to relish it. We knew that it took 10 gallons of sugar-maple sap to make a quart of maple syrup. We ate bitter, mealy acorns because the Paugussett once ate them. We didn't know that you had to put them in boiling water containing wood ash. Nothing, however, compared to the shagbark hickory nuts, despite their nearly impenetrable armor. While mushrooms capture the earthy flavors of autumn, the tight coils of fern fiddleheads taste of the fresh woods coming to life in spring. Some describe the flavor as "grassy," but whereas grass releases green leaf volatiles as an elaborate defense system, ferns produce toxins, requiring that they be cooked for safe eating, like the spring's sought-after morel mushrooms.

I remember swearing off fiddleheads when warnings were issued asserting that they contained a potentially carcinogenic toxin, ptaquiloside. The concern centered on bracken fern, but many now argue that because the heat in cooking them denatures the toxin, the risks are negligible.

Mary often reminds me that plants, like all living things, evolve with their own sophisticated chemical defenses, generally aimed at killing aggressive microorganisms or dissuading creatures from eating them. These very toxins when extracted and administered in carefully calibrated doses supply us with powerful medicines to fight infection, regulate our hearts, and kill our pain.

I began to research foraging courses to fill in the major gaps in my education and experience. Good fortune came my way when my friend Cecilia invited me for a drink at the Café Marly overlooking I. M. Pei's pyramid-entry to the Louvre. We discussed a book she was writing in which she sets out to untangle sordid mysteries in her Polish-Gypsy ancestry, a complex mission given the level of destruction during the Nazi occupation and the cover-ups lingering from the Cold War. Cecilia spends a month each year in the Polish Carpathians, a place where she finds peace with some of her dearest friends and passes time just absorbing the beauty of a landscape that features hilly meadows similar to those of her native Kentucky.

Conversation turned to my own project on wild edibles, and Cecilia had some interesting news to impart.

"You won't believe this," she announced, eyes wide. "Lukasz just wrote a book about eating insects."

"Seriously?"

"I kid you not, Jeff. He's eating bugs."

Cecilia becomes queasy when friends eat steak tartare at restaurants. The thought of eating insects obviously left her aghast. Her friend Lukasz Luczaj is a botanist who runs wild edible workshops out of his hometown of Rzepnik, Poland. Cecilia suggested that I go to one.

Why not? I've never been to Poland, and I assume that the vegetation in the Lower Carpathians is pretty much the same as that found in Burgundy. I read up and discover that Lukasz is a professor of botany and biotechnology of economic plants at the University of Rzeszów. In addition to numerous scientific papers on edible plants and insects, he's written several wild-edible identification guides and cookbooks. Through his papers I'm introduced to ethnobotany and its history, and become increasingly intrigued by what he does.

Lukasz's foraging workshops and cooking classes follow several different formats. Survival purists can choose to live for a week in the woods, feeding themselves only on what can be found there. I opt for the cowards' weekend version—one including eggs, flour, rice, and some condiments.

I send him a query about attending a workshop, and he responds immediately.

"I was planning to do the last workshop on the 22 of September but all the places are full," he writes. "I am just hesitating about putting together another workshop on 20–21 of October (weekend). Would this fit you? I will know for certain in two days."

Lukasz turns out to be exceptionally generous. Because of my special request (and because he knows that I'm Cecilia's friend), he changes his plans and finds enough participants to make it worth his while.

"I will meet you at any time," he e-mails me. "You can also stay later after the workshops for a couple of days if you want to enjoy the area. Things to take: a sleeping bag, carry mat, mug, bowl, spoon, boots, raincoat."

He gives me directions from the two closest airports and is dismayed when I tell him I'll be driving over for the weekend.

"From Paris?" he writes incredulously.

From Paris. I've never been to Prague or Kraków, and, frankly, I've never heard of Tarnów or Rzepnik, only thirty miles from the Ukraine border. I pass through the battlefield at Austerlitz, the spot marked by twenty-foot-tall facsimiles of toy soldiers and an enormous, dumpy-looking cannon. I visit Auschwitz, the bright air and warm autumn sun conspiring to ease the gravity of the experience. The museum quite remarkably receives only two stars as a tourist destination on my map. Two stars for the epicenter of the Holocaust? I drive 1,200 miles in two days from Paris, via Prague and Tarnów, and find myself with a Polish group that includes wilderness-survival buffs, food bloggers, a film producer, and assorted back-to-naturists, including a former judge. All are equipped with cameras and note pads, ancillary to the critical tools for wild food gathering: boots, baskets, spades, and pocketknives. The group had already been out collecting an impressive array of herbs, nuts, and mushrooms.

Lukasz, a solid man with shoulder-length hair and a two-week beard, is busy preparing breakfast in what he calls his "rectangular woks." His stove is a wood fire laid between two logs that support a large sheet of steel mesh over the flame. Everyone is preoccupied with chopping nettles, slicing mushrooms, or picking nearby herbs. Knowing well the perils of mushrooms, I scan for the killers but quickly understand that eating at the workshop would be an act of pure trust. Or should I say faith? The breakfast is delicious, mostly eggs with herbs and mushroom and dead-nettle fritters.

The Lower Carpathians are in the midst of what Americans call Indian summer: deepening yellow foliage with occasional splashes of red, in rolling woods that alternate with a bit of cultivated land. A few docile cows are chained in roadside lots, grazing. Music—Polish traditional songs intermingled with rock and roll—drifts from the lively beginnings of a wedding, which is being held at a pink municipal building that looks like a modest private home.

"Weddings are taken seriously here. They can last three days," a young, brunette food blogger counsels me. "The young people set up a 'passing gate,' and the reception guests must bring a bottle of vodka. You know, kind of like a toll. It's special, no?"

The "passing gate," I'm told, evolved from the old tradition of raising a dowry if the bride happened to be an orphan. The blogger comes from a family with a heather farm, and when she is not helping sell heather, she gives advice on urban foraging and on growing and preparing foods in one's own apartment.

My driving all the way from Paris to attend a workshop in Polish baffles Lukasz. After all, France has many of its own experts on wild edibles. Villages offer tourists wild food festivals, particularly for mushrooms, fruits of the sea, and wild boar. One French wild food guru conducts workshops and runs four restaurants featuring wild edibles. From all accounts, he is getting rich on French weeds. Lukasz is probably thinking: Why come to me when you don't speak a word of Polish? But Lukasz is unique, with interests ranging from researching wild foods in rural China to discover how peasants survived the Great Famine to studying Thai insect cuisine. In between, he's studying traditional foraging knowledge and wild edibles for the twenty-first century. Even the French wild-edibles guru made a pilgrimage to learn from him.

The Carpathians are a 1,000-mile-long range of hills and mountains that crosses parts of Poland, the Czech Republic, Slovakia, Hungary, the Ukraine, and Romania. The mountains are home to boars, bears, wolves, and—perhaps most famously, if fictionally—Transylvanian vampires. To my good fortune and mild sense of shame, everyone speaks English, along with other languages, including Russian. The young blogger, one of the survivalists, and the former Polish judge who got his start painting houses in Chicago take me under their collective wing, interpreting for me when Polish is spoken.

For two days we follow Lukasz, tearing at leaves like goats; yanking up networks of fern root; spading wild garlic, carrots, and parsnips; plucking prickly hips and tart red berries; and pinching off greens that are better known in these parts as "famine food." Famine food was important in the years when the Soviets controlled Poland and guerrilla fighters hid in the woods after the villagers were relocated. There are monuments in the middle of the forest honoring fallen World War II Resistance fighters,

Lukasz Luczaj showing *Trapa natans* (water caultrop), which produces edible nuts (Rzepnik, Poland)

many of whom found ways to nourish themselves in part by what they could forage.

Lukasz strips to his red underwear and wades into a clean pond with a mucky bottom. He must have been doing this from his earliest memory, the way I'd swum in our river in Connecticut. He digs cattail roots with his hands and points out the water chestnuts, a pailful of which he's already collected for the evening meal. "Fishermen hate them," he tells us, and it's easy to see why. It would be like casting into an underwater hedge of brambles.

October is mushroom season. Locals, already satisfied with the rewards of their morning hunt, pour vodka and puff on long cigarette holders, enormous baskets full of cèpes on display. I have never found anything like such a bounty. A fellow participant who works as a film producer had taken a one-and-a-half-hour course in wild-mushroom gathering and exuberantly collects almost everything she can find, Lukasz discarding them nearly as fast as she finds them. Still the basket fills.

All chip in with the washing, chopping, and peeling of our gatherings. The Jerusalem artichokes originally planted in the region by hunters to

Topinambour, cattail roots, and fern roots
(Rzepnik, Poland)

attract deer are particularly difficult to clean. I squat by a brook with a survivalist, who recounts his extreme experiences in Africa. "How do you know what you can collect and eat in Africa?"

"The locals know. They show you."

"You're Polish, so you must know what Lukasz knows about wild edibles. Why are you taking this workshop?"

"It keeps me sharp," he shrugs. In real life, he works in the family business selling machinery, and requires an escape now and again.

I am surprised to learn that we'll be cooking a chicken underground, surrounded by cattail and fern roots as well as the Jerusalem artichokes I've been cleaning. A couple of us spade a small crater while others cut fresh grass and collect firewood and rocks. Lukasz builds a tepee of kindling and firewood, which he sets aflame. Eventually it collapses into the earthen pit, a mass of very hot glowing coals. On top of the coals, Lukasz places rocks, followed by a bed of grass for the chicken, roots, and Jerusalem artichokes, all covered with more grass. Finally, we fill the hole with dirt, letting the chicken steam in grass until the next morning.

Meanwhile, we slice through the putrid, spiny shells of water chestnuts, exposing the sweet, bluish-white inner hemispheres. I've never tasted such wonderful water chestnuts, so different from the nearly flavorless cultivated ones in cans. We peel acorns and set them in boiling water with a few scoops of ashes from the fire, as Lukasz tells us how Native Americans stored acorns in crocks against the advent of hard times. The neighboring wedding moves to an onion-domed church that seems marooned at the end of the road next to a blasted but still-living five-hundred-year-old oak that has produced a substantial crop of fresh acorns.

We are summoned to dinner while rose hips simmer for soup and mushrooms steep for broth. Everyone agrees that the two dishes are truly exceptional. The first is a Thai stew based on thistle leaves, which includes soy sauce, shrimp paste, galangal, tamarind, kaffir lime leaves, and lemongrass. The second is sarma rolls, an ancient Middle European and Middle Eastern dish. Lukasz uses some coltsfoot leaves that we have collected—rather than the more traditional grape or sour cabbage—to wrap a filling of wild onion, rice, and mixed mushrooms. But who knows which ones? Earlier Lukasz accepted some lovely lilac-colored mushrooms that the film producer had picked. He is 99 percent sure he knows what they are, but nevertheless cell-phones the president of the Polish Mycology Society as we stand together fireside. Stars are emerging, and the wedding has cranked up to full blast down the road, no doubt fueled by the vodka dowry. The identity of the mystery mushrooms, it turns out, is *Clitocybe nuda,* indeed edible. The three young women in our group could not be more delighted. They decide the Latin name sounds more like a delicious Italian obscenity and begin chanting *Clitocybe nuda, Clitocybe nuda* over our boiling brews. The dinner conversation ultimately shifts to how many ways potatoes can be eaten.

I have a chance to ask Lukasz how he became interested in botany.

"I've loved plants since I was four, growing up right here," he answers. "It's the structure of plants that fascinated me, the beauty."

He takes me to his office, where he keeps sacks of seeds from meadow flowers. "I collect these seeds from the fields you see around here. People pay to have wildflower seeds."

I can say without exaggeration that this workshop has altered the way I look at plants. It's not simply that the edible species are so abundant and possess impressive medicinal and nutritional properties. I'm now also seeing, through Lukasz's discerning eyes, the architecture of plants from their roots to their leaf patterns. The meals are exceptional, with a wide range of flavors from bitter to sour to sweet to spicy, belying what skeptics might say about wild edibles tasting dull. We learn, too, how our tastes and culinary imaginations are restricted by our own cultures and prejudices. Lukasz tells late-night fireside plant stories in Polish, all but the laughter lost on me.

When I get back to France, I try to identify the edible weeds I encountered in the Carpathians. Plantain, dandelions, mint, nettles, fennel, onion grass, and thyme are everywhere. So are wild carrot and parsnips. Still, I want to make sure I know what I'm doing. Sure enough, after only a little research, I discover that even avid foragers pass up wild carrot for fear of confusing it with deadly hemlock. I must have failed to take in this little complication, though surely we were given emphatic warning, albeit in Polish. I clearly remember digging up wild carrots, rubbing them clean, and gnawing on them with my new Polish friends.

Wild carrots are white rather than orange, and they do taste carroty, though only mildly so. The trouble with them is that they are only good the first year, before they flower. After that it becomes more difficult to distinguish them from hemlock. The leaf structure is slightly different, and they have fuzzy stems and coloration at the base of the stalk. The roots, alas, are almost identical. You have to smell them, and it doesn't seem like a good idea to let a carroty odor alone determine the difference between life and death.

And if wild carrots pose challenges, who knew that sap from wild parsnips can burn if you get it on your skin while exposed to sunlight?

I had been keen on the idea of making wild carrot soup with ginger, wild onions, and tofu, but instead of digging up Queen Anne's lace I ordered wild carrot seeds, along with wild parsnips. I had already planted borage, wild arugula, various Italian kales, and cabbage greens. They all grew beautifully, a garden of lush greens that even the northern Italians might have been proud of if I weren't a sloppy garden tender. Our garden thus became half-wild anyway, weeds cropping up as if by spontaneous generation. One of them made me deeply suspicious. Hemlock? Maybe.

Nevertheless, I dug up my wild carrots, cleaned them, and let Mary smell them.

"They don't smell like carrots to me," she complained.

"Sure they do," I answered heartily. But in truth I doubted myself, and ultimately the wild carrots went unconsumed. I admire Socrates, but not that much.

11

TREE EATERS

DESPITE BEING A pocket-sized Maltese, our dog Snowbell, we have learned over time, is perfectly capable of unzipping luggage and extracting the 85 percent cocoa extra-dark chocolate bars often to be found there, inadvertently poisoning herself and our other four dogs. In a state of alarm that has become all too routine, we call SOS vétérinaire to come save our pack from the toxic effects of caffeine and theobromine, an alkaloid that dogs can't metabolize. Likewise, Brooklyn, our golden retriever and the youngest in the animal tribe, strews our yard with slippers, socks, cushions, expired printer cartridges, and my mother's bras, summarily destroying all plunder. Simply put, our dogs are inveterate thieves.

One evening, while watching a DVD, we heard determined crunching and found Brooklyn with the trademark royal-blue velour Gustave Bernardel Colophane pouch and a semi-circle of amber-colored crystals on the rug, the remains of what had once been the rosin for Mary's cello bow. This latest theft sent us galloping off to do high-speed research on the toxicity of *colophane.*

First we ascertained that European rosin comes from refined *galipot,* the first light sap extracted from select maritime pines, *Pinus pinaster.* While the name *colophane* comes from the name of the ancient Ionian city Colophan in Greece, the southwest of France boasts of the largest maritime pine plantation in Europe. Nineteenth-century engineers designed an enormous forest and drainage network to transform and stabilize pestilent marshlands known as the Landes of Gascony. In those days, the moors were so sodden that residents were obliged to resort to stilts in order to traverse the countryside, look after livestock, plant fields, or just walk into town.

In addition to resin, the forêt des Landes supplies lumber, paper, turpentine, and an array of beauty products, but we've recently learned, courtesy of a National Institutes of Health bulletin, that French maritime pines also serve as a source of Pycnogenol, which helps with circulation problems, allergies, asthma, ringing in the ears, high blood pressure, muscle soreness, osteoarthritis, diabetes, cancer, and—particularly propitious in Brooklyn's case—attention-deficit-hyperactivity disorder. It occurs to me that Brooklyn's consumption of cello rosin may have been a form of self-medication.

Entering the world of edible pine, I found it difficult to extricate myself. Conifers, being evergreen, symbolize eternal life in some northern European Yuletide traditions, particularly German ones. In 1880, Thomas Edison developed strings of lights, and two years later his friend Edward H. Johnson made a splash in the press by wiring up and illuminating his Christmas tree.

To me, pines and cedars, both conifers, have an inherent spirit of peacefulness. The Cedar of Lebanon, firs, and pines are mentioned numerous times in the Bible, and I think the first-named makes the Lebanese flag one of the most appealing among nations. Cedars of Lebanon are known in Arabic as *Horsh Arz el-Rab,* or Cedars of God.

As kids, my brother and I could easily climb to the very top, swaying branches of firs. From the trees near our sitter's house, we could spy on the monastery of the Brotherhood of the Holy Ghost, a mysterious group of gentle men in brown robes whom we often saw on tractors or tending cows. They'd catch us sometimes, usually when we were hiding under pines, and while we remained their "captives," they would show us their gardens or give us a ride on the tractor before gently ejecting us via the front gate. They've remained mysterious in my memory ever since, linked to the smell of pine and something indefinable—the Holy Ghost, perhaps.

This was the era in which Euell Gibbons asked, in a television commercial for Post Grape-Nuts, "Ever eat a pine tree?," thus incurring ridicule from comedians and impersonators forever after. The idea was not just fanciful but, as we now know, dangerous because of the pesticides used to maintain monocultures. Coincidentally, Rachel Carson's profoundly important book *Silent Spring,* which sounded the alert on both pesticides and monocultures, appeared the same year, 1962, as Gibbons's first book, *Stalking the Wild Asparagus.*

Still, conifers provide a key survival resource, particularly in certain areas where they're plentiful but foraging opportunities are scarce. Native Americans valued the trees for their medicinal and nutritional properties. In a famous episode from North American history, an Iroquois brew—most likely made from white cedar with the same health properties as pine, namely a high concentration of vitamin C—saved the crew of the sixteenth-century French explorer Jacques Cartier. After the expedition's ships became encased in ice and snow at the mouth of the Saint Charles River, one-third of the men perished from scurvy and the remaining crew had become sick. In a mere six days, the effect of the Iroquois remedy was deemed a "miracle." No doubt the Iroquois came to regret their compassion. Cartier returned on a second expedition to colonize lands that he had claimed for the king of France fifteen years earlier, lands that were later to become Canada.

Native Americans had many other uses for pine, one being pine-needle pillows. Though they sound like they'd be prickly, the pine in the pillows repels lice and fleas. And what of pine-needle pillow talk, intimate and perfumed as if taking place under the whispering branches of a pine in the breeze? Along these lines, pine incense calms phantoms, foils witches, and prevents bad dreams.

Most importantly for both Indians and explorers, however, pine needles, pinecones, and cambium—the tree's inner living bark—provided food sources. The term Adirondack (meaning "bark eaters"), originally used to describe porcupines (a.k.a. "spine pigs"), became an insulting term that the Iroquois applied to the Algonquians (a.k.a. "spearers of eels and fish"). Winters can be brutally cold in what we now call the Adirondacks, so it's no surprise that the Algonquians took to eating pine trees, considering that the alternatives were either starvation or cannibalism.

Following Brooklyn's newly acquired taste for rosin and imagining her resin-coated teeth, I watched a lengthy discourse on YouTube about how to make pinesap chewing gum. A large sea-scallop shell is heated on a campfire, and hardened pinesap is melted on the shell to refine it as it drips off; then it is mixed with beeswax and honey to create a kind of lava that cools into chewing gum. The process seemed rather laborious just for sweet piney-tasting gum, even if it is all natural and you can swallow it in the end. Who knows, maybe pinesap/honey chewing gum is medicinal.

Honey contains the antibiotic protein defensin; and the malady-fighting powers of Pycnogenol, not to mention pine's vitamin C, may merit the trouble. I even purchased pine honey, exploring the combination in a different direction.

Knowledge acquired from Brooklyn's adventure inspired me to pick fresh spring needles and steep them in boiling water. I wanted to try the brew that had saved Cartier and his remaining men. I found it very pleasant with its Christmasy volatile compound turpene flavoring. Wouldn't kids just intuitively think of brewing pine needles? Probably not. In our orchard, we have four towering Norway spruce, the same type of tree that graces Rockefeller Center each year, a donation that after January 7 is sawed up to make lumber for Habitat for Humanity. The British navy adopted spruce beer to fend off scurvy, although they probably didn't share it with the Indians who inspired it. Norway spruce offers edible twigs and cambium strips to the desperate, though tampering with the inner bark can kill the tree.

Many have heard of Greek retsina, the popular pine-flavored wine that originated in the ancient practice of sealing amphorae with pine resin. Wildcraft folks and Chinese homeopathic medicine advocates proclaim the testosterone-boosting powers of pine pollen, though consumption isn't recommended for male adolescents, who have plenty of testosterone without supercharging themselves.

The pinecone itself, the reproductive structure, is an architectural abstraction of the tree's own form. Over the ages, the pinecone shape acquired its own symbolic meanings, the spiral of the scales representing the "third eye" for ancient Egyptians, Christians, and New Agers alike. In physiology, the pineal gland is pinecone-shaped (thus the name), and because it represents the sole nonbifurcated structure in the brain, it has attracted much conjecture. Descartes maintained that it was the seat of the soul. In fact, it is the seat of melatonin and a good night's sleep.

The beauty of pinecones finds its way into sculpture and décor from the first century (a sixteen-foot-high bronze pinecone is featured in the Vatican's Cortile della Pigna) to Martha Stewart's art of entertaining. But we find even more treasure inside the scales of the pinecone: the seeds we adore in pesto, pastries, stir-fry, couscous, *tajine,* and *furikake.*

Pine nuts have long been considered a delicacy. During my father's days as a hunter-gatherer and impoverished artist, my mother was firmly committed to living beyond our means and would buy them at an exorbitant price. It never occurred to me that I could find pine nuts myself, or that they might have represented a food source for Paleolithic *Homo sapiens* and the Neanderthals before them. Plantations for pine nuts go back to Neolithic settlements, and some Native Americans relied on them as a staple. In the event that you should find yourself faced with starvation, it's good to know that all pine seeds are edible and nutritious, though admittedly it takes some work to make a meal of them. The bottom line is that they qualify as one of the most prized condiments. Who doesn't love crescent cookies with pine nuts?

While exploring the world of pine and *Pinus pinea* in particular, I encountered numerous videos by survivalists, Native Americans, naturalists, and wildcrafters extolling stone pines—also known as umbrella pines—and their cultivation. In one, an irritable Australian rants against imported Chinese pine nuts. Why, he even grew European *Pinus pinea* in his own backyard from a seed he cracked and germinated! He lists a number of remarkable Greek dishes made with pine nuts and goes on to describe the seeds: "That's why they are called a stone pine, look. It looks just like a stone. If you drop it it's like stone too. And if you crack that with a hammer you'll find a pine nut like these ones in the jar. . . . I mean they're so stone, they do look so much like stones, and when you clink them, when you clink them with another one they just sound like stones. Yes, are there more? Yes here's another one. Cockatoos like them."

Thousands and thousands of people watch these videos. What is their appeal? Survivalists can't even decide on the terms: bushcraft or wildcraft. Is it the James Fenimore Cooper Deerslayer-for-a-weekend syndrome? Is it a way of losing oneself in the fantasy of self-reliance? These gurus have one thing in common: they lack charisma. I find something deeply refreshing in their candor. The phrase about the nuts, "They're so stone," kept running through my head, and I decided that I had to grow one.

I knew exactly where a *Pinus pinea* was growing near us, and although we live in Burgundy, far from the Mediterranean, I thought, if there's one already growing here, why not plant another myself? We live near an arboretum and a former National Forestry school that's responsible for a theme highway called the Autoroute des arbres. Travelers are educated about trees as they drive south or pull over to a rest stop featuring a particular species. This, at least, is the theory. The highway exhibits a row of young sequoias just before our exit. I found another stone pine not far from the highway. It wasn't very big, though. Well, if I couldn't grow a large tree, I could at least have a bonsai. Then I'd simply buy Italian pine nuts rather than the suspect Chinese ones, often blamed for the unpleasant pine-mouth syndrome.

As a kid, I planted fruit trees with my father, mainly for the privilege of holding the hose. I still have those images in my head each time I dig and soak a broad hole for a new cherry or apple tree. The idea of growing a stone pine gradually morphed into a grand plan to plant my own arboretum. As the idea was establishing itself in my imagination, Roger Ramon, who taught at the French National School of Forestry, coincidentally phoned us asking if, since he was grafting some fruit trees for himself, he might prepare some for us. My doctor, who introduced us to Roger, started his own orchard with grafted trees, which I found especially appealing. Not only would we have little trees but also we'd have Roger to teach us the art of grafting. He serves as the president of AMAP du Gâtinais, an organization that provides subscribers with a weekly basketful of assorted *bio* vegetables, *bio* being the equivalent of organic in the States. The contents of the baskets vary, challenging household cooks to come up with recipes for vegetables they've never cooked before. It turns out that Roger has become a one-man propagator of grafted fruit trees for his wide circle of acquaintances—a modern-day Johnny Appleseed, if you will.

Roger looks the part of a forester: lean, bearded, sharp-eyed. When we walk in the woods together, he is always pointing out plant and animal behavior in the forest that otherwise I would have missed. He asked us what types and varieties of trees we would like, and we requested twelve: different sorts of pear, apple, cherry, and plum trees. When the rootstock and scions arrived, Roger phoned.

"When would you like to come? We'll graft in the morning and plant the trees in the afternoon."

We arrived the following weekend, and watched him meticulously working his grafting knife, cutting a diagonal line through the rootstock and the scion, the stem of the more desirable variety, which would become the trunk and fruiting portions of the tree. Roger wound paraffin tape around the perfectly matched ovals so that the cells in the vascular cambium would be adjacent and ultimately fuse together. That afternoon we planted the little trees—at this stage, mere twigs—in our kitchen garden, where they would grow for two years before being transplanted.

Years ago we acquired a lovely disused sheep pasture below our orchard, and I decided that this is where I would plant my arboretum, mixing grafted with wild fruit trees, experiments such as the *Pinus pinea* and berry bushes. I know nothing about landscape architecture, but no matter how eccentric my orchard turns out, it seems to me that it will nicer than having three more new tract houses built next to us. I fantasize about creating a miniature organic park, a personalized arboretum that our village one day would appreciate. Roger warned me that deer might amble into the village and level my saplings in a single night. It's hard to imagine, but he assured me it happens. Wild boar and foxes make appearances in town, so why not deer?

It's tricky planting trees. I'd like to be able to see ahead, and I dream about what the saplings will look like in ten, fifteen, twenty years. It's a slow dream, one that requires both time and the tree version of elbowroom, access to the sun. Trees compete to eclipse one other, but they can also develop fascinating symbiotic relationships. In our lower garden, the tallest spruce tree shields one of the largest pear trees I've ever seen from violent windstorms from the west. Meanwhile a beautiful sweet gum tree curves around the other side of the spruce, sprinting skyward for light. It's easy to see why the French manage their forests so carefully to keep them vigorous and productive. While they may have informed instincts, foresters are not simply clairvoyants; they also develop detailed analyses of terrain contours, soil composition, water sources, tree inventories, endangered species, and fire damage.

When at last I acquired stone pine seeds, it was mid-October and the wrong season for planting. I was determined to give it a try, though, so I mail-ordered an indoor grow lamp that glowed with tiny red and blue LED bulbs. Mary declared the lamp to be a "hoax," but I ignored her disdain and installed it under a table. Soon enough, my room in Paris radiated the mysterious light generally associated with the cultivation of marijuana. I followed the video pine-nut guru's advice, fracturing the hard outer shell to help the seed to germinate. I tried a hammer first, and predictably smashed the seed to a pulp. I abandoned the hammer and went for a pair of pliers with an adjustable gap to compensate for my overzealousness. It worked: the pieces of shell fractured and fell away, exposing the edible seeds. Which way to stick them in the soil, though? Thick end up was my guess, and that's what I did.

I was thrilled when after only three weeks a little green hand with its fingers clenched rose out of the soil. Excitedly I showed the sprout to Roger Raymond, who immediately pronounced it *Pinus pinea.*

"How could you possibly know that?"

He mimed the growth, pressing his fingers against his palm and then spreading them.

"They always sprout like this."

I was so pleased that I decided to transport the seedling back and forth from Paris to the country so I wouldn't miss any of its rapid changes in development.

"It's not a pet hamster," Mary reminded me.

To me, though, it was.

12

HERBS, BERRIES, WEREWOLVES, AND VOLCANOES

IT WOULD BE HARD to name a river whose source still remains a mystery. Even the rivulets that feed Guyana's rain-forest-bound Mazaruni River—rife with large black electric eels, piranhas, anacondas, and alluvial gold—were found recently to emanate from the Merume Mountains. Nevertheless, some of us, Mary in particular, look at a river and dream about where it comes from, knowing that to follow it means to be transported to higher land, with a different region and landscape, and to discovery of a different way of life.

Our country house is only twelve miles from the Loire River. At the point nearest us it is already very broad, and in summer long shoals become exposed, serving as a sandy shore for fishermen, swimmers, and statuesque blue herons. Of the great *fleuves,* as the French call them, the large rivers that empty into the Atlantic and the Mediterranean, the Loire is the longest at 1,012 kilometers (632 miles).

Along the river's banks are a number of nuclear power plants, some only a short distance from one another, such as those at Belleville and Dampierre-en-Burly. Not only is the sky crisscrossed with contrails, but the horizon features cloud formations particular to nuclear cooling towers, or "kettles," as we like to call them. They even create their own version of snow squalls during frigid spells in winter.

Despite the string of power plants and urban sprawl along its length, however, the Loire remains one of the world's most beautiful waterways. Near us, it's still clean enough to support a colony of beavers (*castors* in French). A boat tour takes tourists to view beaver footprints on the shore, while the beavers themselves must wonder what all the fuss is about.

One June morning, Mary and I inflate our canoe and paddle down a stretch of the river between La Charité-sur Loire, with its eleventh-century priory, and Pouilly-sur-Loire in the wine region of Sancerre and Pouilly Fumé. We've had the canoe for about a year now, and it's given us an entirely new way to experience the river. We enjoy the variety of birds we encounter, and keep an eye out for the sharp splash of pike and zander feeding on small fish and frogs in the shallows. Naturally, we, too, want to see beavers. Even otter populations are slowly rising with the help of conservationists, but today we content ourselves with watching a few bold nutria cruise across our bow.

We're on the water today because Mary has come up with a plan for a trip to the source of the Loire. Having spent many hours during my childhood gazing into our local stream, I find the idea of this adventure appealing. For our adventure, Mary locates a unique village full of thatched-roofed houses called Moudèyres in the Auvergne, a region in which extinct volcanoes carpeted in green vegetation, and sometimes capped by rocky domes, loom against the sky. Beyond the former coal-mining city of St. Étienne and the deep gorges the Loire cuts between the hills, you arrive at Le Puy-en-Velay, a city known for handmade lace, lentils, and apparitions of the Virgin. Le Puy-en-Velay is stunningly situated around Mont d'Aiguilhe and Mont d'Anis, the remains of two volcanic chimneys. Mont d'Aiguilhe is crowned by an eleventh-century Romanesque chapel, while Mont d'Anis serves as a podium for a fifty-two-foot Rustoleum-colored statue of the Virgin. The enormous statue was created in 1862 by melting and recasting 213 cannons captured at Sebastopol. The Loire curves through the town, which is also dominated by the great Cathedral of Notre Dame. Le Puy is the gateway into a deeply religious countryside.

After Le Puy, the Loire finally enters the high plateaus of Velay and the Mèzenc range, which seems to consist of every possible type of volcano: Hawaiian, Strombolian, Volcanian, and Pelean. The Pelean is formed from the remaining core of an eroded volcano, and the Gerbier du Jonc stands like a huge, dome-shaped anthill with a stream of hikers winding up the steep, rocky trails on one side and descending on the other. Just at the foot of the Gerbier du Jonc, near a farmhouse converted into a tourist rest stop selling artisanal jams and local honey, a watering trough catches a stream of spring water from a pipe in the wall. These are the headwaters of the Loire.

The water leaches westward into a sloping meadow filled with wildflowers and herbs: thyme, marjoram, fennel, rosemary, savory, and other aromatic plants, all the ingredients making up what is now popularly known as *herbes de Provence*. Traditionally, locals picked and dried herbs, mixing them for flavoring sausages, roasts, and stews. In local stores we discover specialty herbal mixtures intended to facilitate sleep, digestion, relaxation, and physical and mental healing.

Our hotel restaurant, the Pré Bossu in nearby Moudèyres, is notable not just for its rustic basalt façade and authentic thatched roof but also for its extensive gardens, the most impressive of which stretches below the parking area to the edge of a pasture. It serves as a vast kitchen garden with herbs and vegetables planted in a diamond pattern, the produce used for the chef's exceptional cuisine. Two greyhounds languish in the reception area, looking very much as if they had been designed by Giacometti rather than bred to run down rabbits. Each of the hotel's six rooms is named after a different local bird.

Madame Moreels, who runs the Pré Bossu with her husband, Monsieur Grootaert, the chef, tells us the dogs' names: "Xeres, like the vinegar, or better, what one calls sherry. The other is Uto—U-t-o." The latter is a made-up name, like a planet in science fiction. Madame Moreels, fortyish, red hair tied tightly back like a dancer's, has a natural attractiveness and grace to go along with her firm ideas. At the entry by the hotel desk stands a massive glass cabinet filled with *confiture* and chutneys, many of which incorporate unexpected herbs and wildflower flavorings.

"Oh, you know, it's just sugar and fruit," says Madame, but concedes, "I have three hundred recipes. The wild berries, flowers, and herbs are the treasures of our region, and I put them to good use."

The restaurant working on the farm-and-garden-to-plate principle remains open only from late spring to October. The daily menu features two selections: vegetarian and nonvegetarian.

The village of Moudèyres itself has an interesting story. An aviator named René-Pierre Neuville, who helped organize the logistics for the Allied landing at Casablanca in 1942, was years later expelled from Algeria, as were many other *pieds noirs*. During his wanderings through

France, he discovered the ruined village of Moudèyres. He personally mobilized the inhabitants to renovate their own town, house by house, as a communal effort.

In a pasture just behind the Eco Ferme Perrel, Moudèyres holds its small annual fair on August 15, an important French holiday honoring the ascension of the Virgin Mary. The main event of the fair is the *repas campagnard,* a country feast. Three large cast-iron cauldrons with their own wood-burning chambers and chimneys are lined up along a stone wall. Out of curiosity, I ask one of the organizers for the cabbage soup recipe, a fixture of all country fairs in the region. He points to an old man in a green-striped summer shirt, who was *bien arrosé*—well watered, as the French say—at the wine bar. "I'm not a cook. It's just bacon, potatoes, and cabbage."

"And a broth?"

"Well, of course, but I'm not a cook."

"Did you know Neuville?"

"The aviator? I certainly did. I put up that plaque for him. I was the mayor here for forty-two years. I worked with Neuville to change Moudèyres, and it took me twenty years to teach people to pick up their own trash."

For dinner Monsieur Grootaert prepares a rabbit ballotine, the light loin meat rolled around a pâté of prunes with gelatin and garden herbs. The lightness of the rabbit with synergetic sweet herbal mix is excellent, redolent with the essence of the landscape.

It seems to be the case that when you get older you often find yourself back in summer camps, either as a participant or a teacher. Mary always goes to a summer music camp, often the oldest participant among young people preparing for the conservatory. The camps that she chooses happen to be in Haute-Loire or farther south in la Lozère, so after our Moudèyres experience, we now find ourselves every year back in the general region of herbs, berries, rivers, and volcanoes. One music camp in la Canourgue is held in a *pisciculture* school that rents its space while fish-farming students are on summer break. The fish dart about in their tanks to the strains of Haydn, Beethoven, and Bartók. In addition to the Loire, many of the great French rivers originate in Auvergne, including the Lot, Allier, Ardèche, Hérault, and Dordogne. In la Canourgue, which

Dan Gunn and Olivia Baes enjoying smoked trout with wild greens and mixed berries (Paris)

has crystal-clear, trout-filled streams passing right through the town, the commune has established a special *parcours de pêche,* a fishing run that is reserved for the handicapped.

If you have any compulsion to fish, this area of France is irresistible. The Allier, one of the few uncorrupted rivers in Europe, is said to contain wild salmon, though the fish must be released in the unlikely event that anyone should catch one. When Mary's music camp finishes, we generally rent a basalt stone house in a farming village called Ouides situated between the Loire and the Allier Rivers, which in places are only fifteen miles apart. It's an easy walk through a forest to a seemingly bottomless, clear volcanic crater lake called Lac du Bouchet.

Like many kids growing up in the country, I fished, though I was a far more productive diver. Success largely depends on the angler's ability to read the water. Is it too warm or too high, too early or too late; are you using the right fly or nymph? One needs Zen training in order to cope with the inevitable tangles and snags that seem to work by their own rules of physics. I think just getting the tippet end through the eye of a fly hook is a triumph, myself. My fishing pal Frédéric insists that French trout, surviving anglers over the millennia, are simply smarter through natural selection than American trout, which only needed to dodge osprey, otters, and brown bears. Perhaps he's right.

Once, in my determination to find an underfished bend in the Allier, I parked my car at a small turnoff before a viaduct and edged my way down a precipitous cliff side to a perfect river pool, only to discover a human-sized skeleton sprawled across the rocks. Apparently someone either had fallen or was tossed from the edge of the viaduct and hadn't been discovered until the very moment I appeared on the scene. Surveying the parched ribs, hipbones, and denuded skull, I experienced a Raymond Carver *Short Cuts*–type dilemma: Should I go to the *gendarmerie* and spend what would undoubtedly be hours reporting a death, or should I maybe just fish for graylings and trout a little while first? On closer inspection, I decided the bones belonged to a star-crossed lamb rather than a child. Dilemma solved. I fished for an hour while standing on a ledge with the skeleton.

The experience brought to mind Thoreau's rhapsodic passage on a dead horse, and his celebration of death as a vision of the great engine of life. The wise man rejoices in the presence of death, the cycle through which creatures and ultimately plants derive nourishment: "I love to see that Nature is so rife with life that myriads can be afforded to be sacrificed and suffered to prey on one another; that tender organizations can be so serenely squashed out of existence like pulp—tadpoles which herons gobble up, and tortoises and toads run over in the road; and that sometimes it has rained flesh and blood!" This famous passage strikes me as an odd exultation from the vegetarian Thoreau, although he once admitted he'd eat a fried rat if he had to in order to survive. Ultimately Thoreau aims his message against compassion, and considering that most of us keep meat in our refrigerators we'd appear foolish to argue with him. Whitman shares a less gory vision in "A Child Says, What Is the Grass?":

> All goes onward and outward . . . . and nothing collapses,
> And to die is different from what any one supposed, and luckier.

From the ledge, I spotted a rowan tree with clusters of brilliant red berries and a compound pinnate leaf structure. I decided on the spot that of course I must plant a rowan or two in my arboretum, even though they proliferate throughout France. They have lovely white flowers in the spring, edible berries, and orange-red leaves in autumn. The sweet-scented flowers lure pollinating insects, and the berries attract birds, even to their demise, particularly if they happen to be a waxwing or a thrush, being prized by hunters. A rowan branch held in the right hand can serve as a divining stick for finding precious metals. The tree can be used for practicing witchcraft if necessary. Emerson and Thoreau would have found the rowan tree innately divine even without the supernatural perks.

So who wouldn't want a *Sorbus aucuparia,* particularly in the Haute-Loire and la Lozère, which seem to have more than their fair share of ghosts and terrorizing beasts? Werewolves and witches tend to impose themselves in sparsely inhabited French regions, and la Lozère is one of the least-populated parts of Europe. In the latter part of the eighteenth century, these were the reputed hunting grounds for the insatiable Bête du Gévaudan, a real creature searching for its own sort of wild edibles; over two hundred attacks allegedly left more than a hundred men, women, and children dead. While the beast was thought to have been a wolf or a hybrid wolfdog, its mystery has never been solved.

Scrambling up the embankment, I noticed in the shaded areas mixed with moss a kind of ground cover with leaves and berries that somewhat resembled the blueberry bushes *Vaccinium corymbosum* that grew in our woods in New England. These, however, are the far lower, smaller, darker *Vaccinium myrtillus,* also known as bilberry. Bilberries can be found in practically every market, but here they are in the wild—*myrtilles,* as the French call them—and I could see that the forest was carpeted with them. On the slope I also found several fresh cèpes and a handful of orange chanterelles.

On my return to Ouides, I eagerly discussed my finds with our ninety-year-old neighbor Mr. Hervé, who sells us potatoes and string beans. He's lived his entire life in the village, raising his family while working as a baker out of his home. He showed us the wood-fired ovens he'd start up each day at 4:00 a.m., filling the town with the rich odor of bread that signaled morning just as surely as did the sound of church bells.

I showed him my cèpes and chanterelles, and he nodded, unimpressed, before saying, "The ground has been too dry for mushrooms. There are no mushrooms this year."

I was holding them right in front of him! I knew better than to show him my *myrtilles,* hardly a novelty for him in any case.

The year after what I now think of as the skeleton fishing trip, Mary learns from her cello teacher's wife, a nurse, that care should be taken when foraging in the Haute-Loire. Fox urine can carry a parasite that triggers alveolar echinococcosis, a nasty disease affecting the liver and other organs. Its symptoms may appear as much as a year after the victim is infected. The general rule is not to pick and eat anything from a height lower than the waist in "black zones," the Haute-Loire department being one. For all I know, cysts may be forming in my organs this very minute from all the *myrtilles* I've already eaten.

My greatest pleasure in Ouides is walking the dogs on the farm roads all the way to the forest surrounding Lac du Bouchet. One morning not long after my discussion with Monsieur Hervé, we boldly penetrate the late-summer haze clinging to the fields to break into sunny higher ground, where one already senses the shift in seasons. Red raspberry hedges sometimes entwined with blackberries line the tractor road, along with cow parsley, elder, juniper, oak, poppies, roses, rowan, wild carrot, and numerous edible greens. Far below us, ground fog erases the Gorge d'Allier. We reach the edge of the forest in bright sunlight where a fox briefly glares at us before vanishing. The three dogs and I approach near her den and find several holes not far from enormous parasol mushrooms. It has rained for a couple of days, and with the moisture, mushrooms have instantly popped up everywhere. Strangely, however, many in the forest have been knocked over and destroyed. On closer examination, I see that the stalks have been chewed into fine bits. Mystery solved: wild boar squabble somewhere in trees, launching the dogs into fits of hysterical barking.

A weasel-like animal leaps out of a stone wall and just as suddenly vanishes, only to reappear and disappear and reappear again. Pop goes the weasel—or ermine, or marten. Whatever it is, it's amusing itself. In all likelihood it is a *fouine* (beech marten). A neighbor in Burgundy says that they are impulsive killers, showing us fang marks on the pheasant he brought us as a gift. We are grateful for gifts, of course, but this was a little like someone giving you roadkill.

That afternoon, Mary and I inflate the canoe and launch it on Lac du Bouchet, a circular body of water created by a volcanic eruption, now fed primarily by rainwater. Mary trolls her feet through cold water that is more than three hundred feet deep, and a trout pops to the surface glare. At night the lake glimmers with stars, inverted constellations under which I imagine crayfish prowling. The native endangered ones here are known as *écrevisses à pattes blanches,* literally, crayfish with white feet. I'm reminded of my night dives, how creatures emerge in the starry darkness. But above all, I wonder what evolutionary purpose the white feet served.

13

THE CHARMED POT

WHEN I WAS IN Poland for my workshop with Lukasz Luczaj, botanist and wild edibles expert, I spent some time watching dragonflies "copter" stone to twig, reed to reed. Lukasz later described how in Thailand it is customary to angle for dragonflies by winding the tip of a stick with spider web. The image struck me as natural and poetic, exploiting the dragonfly's inclination to alight on rushes and using spider-spun adhesive for entrapment. The Balinese, who savor dragonflies, sweep them out of the air with a palm frond coated with a sticky fruit extract. Then they dewing and flash-fry the captured dragonflies in coconut oil. While most Americans and Europeans have yet to add dragonfly cuisine to their culinary repertoire, they can enjoy a taste at insectarium cafés or Bugfest stalls. Dragonflies, or "pond hawks," as certain species are commonly known, rank high on insect menus.

The mere suggestion of fishing for flying things and the culture of strange foods evokes Washington Irving's indelible description of fly-fishing for swallows from the towers of the Alhambra.

> I had repeatedly observed a long lean fellow perched on the top of one of the towers, manoeuvering two or three fishing-rods as though he were angling for the stars. I was for some time perplexed by the evolutions of this aërial fisherman, and my perplexity increased on observing others employed in like manner on different parts of the battlements and bastions; it was not until I consulted Mateo Ximenes, that I solved the mystery.
>
> It seems that the pure and airy situation of this fortress, has rendered it, like the castle of Macbeth, a prolific breeding-place for swallows and martlets, who sport about its towers in myriads, with

> the holiday glee of urchins just let loose from school. To entrap this bird in the giddy circlings, with hooks baited with flies, is one of the favourite amusements of the ragged "sons of the Alhambra."

Mary read this passage to me while we sat by the fountains at the Alhambra's Garden of Arif, swallows everywhere, and I am still appalled by it. Both of us feel a close affinity for swallows. My mother raised their unfortunate fallen nestlings, feeding them fishing-bait maggots. The parent swallows are among the most beautiful harbingers of spring, with their breathtaking insect-devouring dives and fountain-sipping swoops. They become our summer companions and nest in our stable. They swarm for their autumn departure, and then the very same ones return the following spring, flying through the house and considering nesting sites above the hot-water heater or in my mother's closet.

The Chinese use swallows' nests, the hardened saliva adding rare delicate flavor to their cherished soup. Are the swallows themselves edible, though? If you've read Isaak Walton's classic *Compleat Angler,* you know the answer is yes, for he includes a discussion of Italian swallow fishing from steeples. Sir Henry Wotton, seventeenth-century diplomat, poet, and author especially knowledgeable about Italy, assured Walton that swallow meat was excellent. I'm doubtful. Swallow meat has a bad ring, something like hummingbird steak.

What is extreme or exotic to one culture hardly raises an eyebrow in another. You might not expect a challenging culinary experience in the cosmopolitan hub of Singapore, but in steamy, 100-degree heat at the fulcrum of the Northern and Southern Hemispheres we once visited the Chinatown "wet market" (meaning hose-washed concrete market floors) near the Sri Miramman Temple. The market resembled a multilevel parking lot, with colorful foods and clothing from all over the world. On the lowest level, fish lay hacked up into chunks, the heads sold separately for the revered fish-head curry, while black eels writhed in a pile with nowhere to go but over, between, and through each other. Enormous frogs stood statuesque in woven bamboo waiting to be claimed, and turtles trudged around glumly in basins. The live crustaceans foamed and shifted, shell to shell. Mary nearly passed out from the heat and smell. I took her out to Jurong Lake, where practically no one was around and she could stand on a bridge and recover while watching kingfishers pick fish out of their own speedy iridescent reflections. Monkeys followed a woman into the restrooms: we expected her to come rushing out, but instead the monkeys emerged casually, trailing toilet paper.

The Singapore "wet markets" provide food products for a broad spectrum of culinary traditions—Hindu, Muslim, and Christian. I didn't investigate the Chinese passion for extracts and powdered remedies that include so many endangered species. But certainly swallow saliva maintains a presence there in one form or another. The Chinatown wet-market experience transported me kettleside to Macbeth's witches:

> Fillet of a fenny snake,
> In the cauldron boil and bake;
> Eye of newt and toe of frog,
> Wool of bat and tongue of dog,
> Adder's fork and blind-worm's sting,
> Lizard's leg and owlet's wing,
> For a charm of powerful trouble,
> Like a hell-broth boil and bubble.
> ALL: Double, double toil and trouble;
> Fire burn and cauldron bubble.
> Third Witch: Scale of dragon, tooth of wolf,
> Witches' mummy, maw and gulf
> Of the ravin'd salt-sea shark,
> Root of hemlock digg'd i' the dark

I always wondered what the weird sisters did with the brew in the "charmed pot." Maybe someone could open an exotic food restaurant, call it "Weird Sisters," and franchise it. Stranger things have been done.

Some foods, like grasshoppers, are such common treats in Mexico and other parts of the world that friends report crunching on them like potato chips. My friend Jean-Pierre, however, writes from Kinshasa, "The people offer me termites on a stick, but I say no, no. Please, they are for you." Kinshasa's Gambela market offers Congolese termites alongside weevil larvae, caterpillars, grasshoppers, and other such delicacies. For the really adventurous diner, tour promoters have put together extreme-cuisine insect itineraries allowing the traveler to consume centipedes, scorpions, and sizable grubs while taking in the Asian sights.

In May 2013, the United Nations Food and Agriculture Organization encouraged gourmet cooks and food writers to find ways to make insects more appetizing because they are a sustainable protein source. What's the point, one might ask? Ground up and mixed with anything, who would know the difference? The U.S. Food and Drug Administration has already established acceptable limits for insects in wheat flour and tomato products. Including insects in your diet is not nearly as dangerous as using animal brains as a filler/binder for hamburger, the prions potentially leading to transmissible spongiform encephalopathies, mad cow disease being one of its forms.

With starvation a problem all over the world, encouraging people to consume insects makes sense. While we were sitting around the fire at his wild edibles workshop, Lukasz commented that the UN will "ruin" edible insects if it instigates large-scale insect farming rather than using insects from the wild. We'll end up feeding insects on corn and giving them antibiotics and growth hormones.

Let me be frank. Eating insects, larvae, and worms doesn't appeal to me, despite arguments that some hardly differ from other exoskeleton animals such as shrimp, lobsters, and crayfish. Granted, a scorpion shares certain characteristics with a crayfish, but the resemblance doesn't translate into culinary appeal. When I was a kid, my brother and I used to announce to one another that everything chocolate-coated potentially contained an insect or spider, grubs and black widows topping the list. We were not about to let a raisin simply pass for a raisin in gross-out contests. Who knew that one day experts might consider insects the "food of the future"?

We now compare termites to cows as sustainable food sources. Of course, there may well be religious food taboos to be respected. Locusts appear to be halal, but I'm not sure about other insects. Certain Bible passages give the green light: "Yet these may ye eat of every flying creeping thing that goeth upon all four, which have legs above their feet, to leap withal upon the earth" (Leviticus 11:21).

The point is to face the future: insect, larvae, and worm; culinary experience or duty.

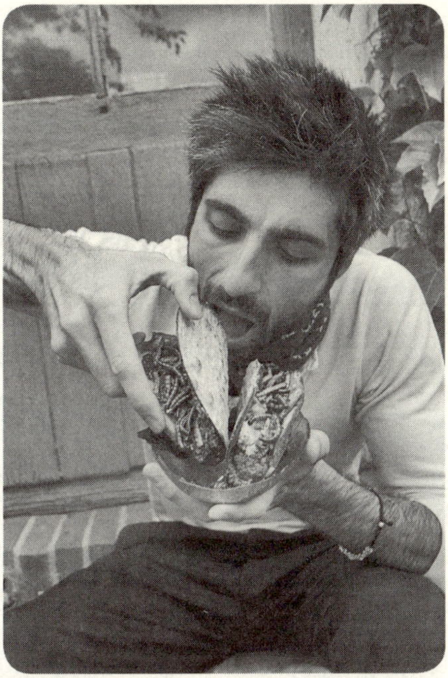

Chauncey Alan attacking a worm-and-peppers taco (Rogny-les-Sept-Écluses, Burgundy)

Mary says, "If you eat a worm in a piece of fruit or a mushroom, what's the difference? The worm is the fruit. We inadvertently eat insects and worms all the time."

Okay, that's rational enough. But inadvertent consumption is as far as most will go, including Mary. In addition to cultural differences, there are primal mechanisms in us that dictate what's appetizing based on principles of survival. Thus, babies and children tend to go for white foods, and many people instinctively dislike bitter tastes. Bitterness is a trait common to toxins.

Other categories may exist when it comes to insects. Queasy neophytes might start with scorpion vodka or mescal when embarking on scorpion and maguey-worm culinary experiences. In Mexico, maguey worms are not only found pickled at the bottom of mescal bottles but are sold in markets and are consumed in tacos—or alive. With enough sliced chilies, garlic, and dried shrimp, the maguey worms might not be too bad. When it comes to eating scorpions, anesthesia might seem the best option, but it's easy to find recipes for them fried or in soups or on tapas. Intellectually, I grasp the idea of eating worms, grubs, grasshoppers, and termites because they are plentiful. And some are so annoying that it's gratifying to find ways to get back at them.

I taught a graduate fieldwork writing course with an anthropologist who specializes in taste of place. Specifically, she studies the culinary customs in Belleville, a neighborhood of northern Paris that includes Egyptians, Tunisians, Algerians, Turks, Chinese, Vietnamese, Sephardic Jews, Congolese, Hindus, and even some old working-class French. It has been called a "mosaic" of cohabiting strangers, and these groups maintain not only their languages but their most common foods. What we end up discussing is a mosaic of delicious and diverse cuisines that are characteristic of a very lively neighborhood. What you find in Belleville is not always the true opposite of weird-sisters food but seems possible, even good—fried duck feet and head; Sichuan pig ears. Encouraged, I try to interest my anthropologist friend in eating some insects with me. Someone in Belleville must do it. They certainly eat everything else.

"I read about this place called Le Festin Nu," I tell her. "They serve fried beetles, grilled grasshoppers, and silkworms. We should try it."

"Look," she says. "I'm willing to eat insects, but only if they're served in an authentic fashion. Le Festin Nu? That's just dare food."

I am disappointed, obviously, but I can't argue with her logic. Wistfully, I imagine groups of laughing young people, scorpions filling their mouths, gathered in a place named after William Burroughs's *Naked Lunch.* I decide not to bring up Chez Mushi, another possibility. The Japanese have a venerable insect-consumption tradition, especially in the Shinshu and Tohoku regions, where rice-field grasshoppers and bee and wasp larvae are popular. Indeed, rice-field grasshoppers are so popular they have become scarce.

I take the plunge, though it's a timid plunge. I don't go into my backyard and chase down grasshoppers, crickets, and larvae. Instead, I delve into the bug-eating experience the modern way: by acquiring them on the Internet. I can't simply look at a bug or worm in the wild and muster the enthusiasm to eat it. I reason that, for my inaugural insect-eating experience, Internet-purchased bugs might be the safest to eat and provide the greatest variety. The Mexican and the Japanese recipes I've found sound the most palatable, so that's what I'll concentrate on.

It's surprisingly easy to purchase edible bugs and worms. Critical to my starter package is the bottle of scorpion vodka for anesthetic purposes. The other ingredients include silk and bamboo worms, two types of crickets, grubs, and grasshoppers. I'm afraid I might have more difficulty tracking down dried ancho and *pasilla* peppers in Paris, but my mother's favorite *épicerie,* Izraël in the Marais, carries almost every kind of spice, dried fruit, vegetable, and exotic canned good that you could possibly want.

Mary is excited about the garlic, pepper, and shrimp tacos. The first time I had them was in the back of a camper at the Matagorda Bay Nature Park—a place where Nicaraguan immigrants from Houston seemed to be netting everything that crawled or swam in the tide at night. We could have cooked their catch and put it in our tacos, too, since the garlic and pepper mixture was so delicious.

"You aren't going to put worms in this, are you?" Mary asks worriedly.

"I have to. That's the recipe."

"You don't *have* to do anything. Just keep them separate. You can have your worm tacos, and I'll make my tacos the way I want them."

"They're not worms, they're grubs."

"Same thing."

We sit down at the table, I with a separate pan of flash-fried grubs next to me. The key to eating insects, I've decided, is to mask the flavor and texture, and to be slightly drunk. The excellent flavor of the grub tacos surprises me to such a degree, however, that I end up eating the larvae straight from the pan. They have a light nut flavor. This encouraging experience and more scorpion vodka leads to subsequent meals of sautéed crickets with soy and sake on shreds of Chinese cabbage, a slice of avocado, a few gratings of carrot, and toasted sesame seeds. The rest of my bugs go into sweet soy grasshopper and grub sushi.

Despite my modestly successful foray into insect cuisine, the anthropologist's point about taste of place being contingent on customs makes an impression on me. Even if certain traditional foods don't win you over, experiencing them in Japan and Mexico would be enriching. I live in France, so what wild edibles cuisine is most identified with Burgundy but still might qualify as weird-sisters food? "Toe of frog" goes into the hell-brew, and in Burgundy *cuisses de grenouilles,* or frog legs, are considered a delicacy that conjures up family times. Even the great cookbook writer Jacques Pepin turns sentimental over memories of catching frogs with his brother in Burgundy.

We had enormous bullfrogs in New England, but it never occurred to us to eat them. My first experience eating frog legs was in the surreal early-morning hours in Rungis, purported to be the world's largest wholesale food distribution hub. In the dead of night Rungis bustles, and I needed a special invitation from friends in the food industry to even enter. Platters appeared on which traditional sautéed frog legs—coated with parsley, garlic, and butter—were arranged in a star pattern. Years later, in Louisiana, I had them spicy Creole style, french-fried along with alligator sausage. The flavor is often compared with that of chicken, though frog legs have a more delicate taste and consistency, and alligator is much denser. I think it would be spectacular to have a Cajun, Creole, and Burgundian alligator cook-off. I've wondered if alligator qualifies as forage food. Why not, if one is coming out of a marsh after your little dog?

When it comes to the consummate Burgundian wild edible, nothing trumps the *Helix pomatia* (also known as *gros-blanc*) or *Escargot de Bourgogne.* While snail slime is not on the witches' list, most who are unaccustomed to eating snails would probably consider them appropriate ingredients for a vile brew. Psalms 58:8 takes snail slime to the ultimate: "May they [the wicked] be like a slug that melts away as it moves along, like a stillborn child that never sees the sun." Remarkably, snails produce mucus from eight different kinds of glands. The mucus we see in silvery trails provides all-terrain traction, particularly over rough ground, but more importantly it helps the snail adhere to vertical surfaces. Mucus protects vulnerable soft tissue from drying out. Snails also secrete mucus that dries to form an epiphragm, a hardened enclosure that shields them in dormant periods such as during drought or hibernation. Snail slime has been used in a variety of remedies, primarily for skin ailments, since antiquity, and more recently the cosmetic industry has exploited it as an anti-aging agent in certain creams because of its collagen, glycolic acid, and antibiotic content.

The snail is a gastropod with a single lung, and moves via muscular

Helix pomatia or *gros-gris,* the escargot,
symbol of Burgundy cuisine
(Rogny-les-Sept-Écluses, Burgundy)

undulations of its foot. It has eyes at the end of an upper pair of tentacles, and two lower smaller tentacles for smell and other senses. Somehow this arrangement inspires cartoonists to portray them as endearing rather than weird. Perhaps no one prized *Helix pomatia* for remedies and cuisine as much as the Romans. They may be known as escargot in Burgundy, but they are also known as Roman snails as far north as Latvia.

The escargot has long been a symbol of regional Burgundian cuisine from the smallest village bar to a Michelin-starred restaurant. Before the days of nouvelle cuisine, a classic meal included a dozen escargot followed by coq au vin, cheese, and dessert. If your stomach could handle it, you'd be five pounds heavier the next day. Famous cooks in Burgundy offer their numerous alternatives for the traditional *escargot de Bourgogne* with parsley butter by developing *croustillants, ragoûts, fricassées, fritons,* and *feuilletés* using snails. One special dish from the eat-your-backyard genre of cooking is *escargot aux orties,* snails with nettles.

Because of both the popular consumption of *Helix pomatia* and the effect of pesticides on its population, collecting is now controlled, and a large percentage of the snails being consumed are *Helix aspersia* (*petit-gris*), a species that, unlike the *Helix pomatia,* can be easily farmed. Four *héliciculture* farms exist within fifty miles of us, producing snails in the hundreds of thousands, mainly *petit-gris* and a North African cousin, *Helix aspersa maxima,* or *gros-gris.*

One day my mother announces, "I have a snail recipe I want to try."

"But you never eat snails!"

"It's a soup. Snails, green chilies, and Udon. I have it written down. I'll show you."

"Okay," I say, "but let's use the ones in the garden. Mary's at war with them anyway."

"I need fifty of them. Look for them around the planters. That's where they sleep all day."

"Then what?"

That's the big problem: none of us know whether to starve them, feed them, or just let them hang in a net sack. We know to avoid giving them toxic plants, but how do we protect ourselves from what snails have been eating? At a yard party, I ask a contractor friend, Jean-Marie Boisgibault, a sturdy Frenchman and president of the local branch of the Federation of Hunters, how he prepares the escargot he collects. His lively wife, Evelyne, interrupts, "Prepare escargot? That's too disgusting! We get them frozen at Picard."

"But I've seen Jean-Marie collecting them along the road."

"He does it for friends."

Jean-Marie nods, remaining mute on the topic.

Okay, it's much easier to buy escargot prepacked in butter and garlic at a fish store or Picard, which admittedly sells high-quality frozen food. The great French restaurants use canned escargot. But I'm determined to go through the traditional process of cleaning and feeding the snails myself.

Just as my mother suggested, snails cluster under the herb pots and around the strawberry planters. We read that we should put them into a container with firm mesh since snails possess Herculean strength for their size. My mother supplies them with cornmeal, thyme, and water, and quite remarkably the snails immediately deploy, searching out escape routes. In a few days when all else fails, they secrete mucus to form an epiphragm.

They're all dead!" I announce.

"What?" my mother says incredulously.

"I threw them in the mulch bin."

"They were hibernating," my mother retorts. "They sure outsmarted you."

Some chefs say that the best time to collect snails is in the spring after they emerge and feed on fresh greens; others argue that snails fattened over the summer provide the best flavor. For better or worse, I have to settle for the latter, having only October before the snails seek winter quarters. The first snail pen was too prisonlike, so on my second try I provide more shelter in the form of wooden lean-tos, and more humidity and dark by covering the pen with cloth. Balancing the pen at a slight tilt provides a more natural source of water, a snail village with its own pond. This is how I leave them.

Returning to the country, I find that the snails have organized a way to force the wire top loose and escape again. We only have a handful left. This latest development transforms our attitude toward snails to a sober respect. We watch them with sympathy, as did Shakespeare in *Venus and Adonis:*

> . . . as the snail, whose tender horns being hit,
> Shrinks backward in his shelly cave with pain,
> And there, all smother'd up, in shade doth sit,
> Long after fearing to creep forth again

Even Mary is won over. After two weeks of feeding, starving, and cleansing snails, I find that I've become attached to them, admiring their eye-stalk tentacles, their tenacious if vulnerable grasp on dark and humid earth, their sensitivity. Nevertheless, I've come this far, and I intend to finish the job. The next step is to purge the slime from their bodies by putting them on kosher salt and vinegar, but Mary vigorously protests, "That's too cruel." And indeed, I learn later that groups exist to protect snails from such inhumane treatment.

Jacques Pepin contends that this purging step is a mistake because the muscle becomes tougher. I don't know whom to believe. My plan is to boil the snails, remove them from their shells, and then cook them again for a couple of hours in a special seaweed court bouillon. In deference to snail activists, however, I numb them in the freezer before boiling them.

"Since this is the first time I've done this, I'm just going to prepare them in the classic Burgundian fashion," I say to Mary.

"Okay," she agrees, and helps me with the preparations. After two hours of brewing the snails, I sauté them in fresh butter, garlic, and parsley. They were worth the fuss: We'd never had more tender, flavorful escargots, and they'd come from our own garden, too. No wonder snails don't make it in the weird sisters' ingredient list. Witches, in general, are not in the business of haute cuisine.

14

ODDS AND ENDS

TWICE A WEEK for more than two decades, I have run the same ten kilometers of country road from Rogny-les-Sept-Écluses to Aillant-sur-Milleron and back. For most joggers, this lack of variety would amount to some kind of epic punishment. To me, though, the landscape has gradually become indistinguishable from myself. Ideas, poems, stories, recipes come to me differently than they do in my study. Maybe the rhythm of running and the endorphins the body releases influence the working of the mind. Certain passages from audio books will haunt a copse or a pasture. One stretch open to cultivated fields and the broad sky will forever belong to wounded Andrei Bolonsky's transcendental vision in the battle of Austerlitz: "'What's this? Am I falling? My legs are giving way,' he thought. . . . 'how differently do those clouds glide across that lofty infinite sky! How was it I did not see that lofty sky before? And how happy I am to have found it at last! Yes! All is vanity, all falsehood, except that infinite sky. There is nothing, nothing, but that.'" My quest to learn about wild edibles would bring me to the very battlefield that Tolstoy describes, and I believe I have seen the same sky, felt the same feelings just lying on my back and looking up.

The country road has become a measure of the seasons. On the edges of drainage ditches, ice forms, rice-paper thin and nearly invisible on the fermented leaves and sweet cattail roots. When water drains into the field, a sheet of ice remains, blades of grass imprinted on it. Underneath the ice is the raw mud and the nude winter of things. Frost sparkles on mint, plantain, *pissenlit,* wild carrot. Both edible and inedible weeds are as beautiful as anything the florist sells. In winter, I sometimes find a snail, *Helix pomatia,* in deep hibernation, the opening of its shell sealed with a protective covering. From spring to autumn, though, after a night rain, the snails lay their own slick over the asphalt. One could collect a meal in minutes. Cacophonous frogs can be heard from pond to pond in spring, while hares become bolder seeking mates. They will lope down the road for a half kilometer before tearing off across a field of sprouting winter wheat. Lapwings make their nests in the fields, and I am reminded that the Vicomte de Mauduit advocated snatching their eggs, reasoning that the farmers would just destroy them with their machinery. I suppose one could eat the eggs of any wild bird—partridges, ducks, geese, seagulls—but I'm not attracted to the idea.

Sometimes on my runs, the medevac arrives in the village, a white helicopter that comes to transport someone for emergency medical treatment. We live too far from the medical centers for ambulances in such emergencies. Often those transported out have never flown in a helicopter before; many have hardly left the village, "a life in the shadow of the steeple," they call it. The charms of the capital are lost on them. "They'd have to drag me to get me to Paris," one will tell another. Many from the generations with traditional knowledge of wild edibles, however, have left us, never to return.

Because the medevac lands so close to our home, on takeoff one might get a bird's-eye glance of my wild edibles projects. The borage completely overruns the kitchen garden now and is starting to grow in the lawn. Sorrel crops up in heady bunches, and wild garlic and parsnips occupy a significant patch. *Agretti* finally grows after three tries, though it is fibrous, lacking the salty crunch of the Ligurian variety. If you visited, you'd see on the terrace wall a pot containing wild asparagus along with wild cherry and *Pinus pinea* seedlings. Yes, I became greedy. Down below the old orchard with the chickens and the prayer path, black plastic film has been laid to kill the grass in a pasture, and to attract worms that will aerate the soil in preparation for grafted trees and the wild-edibles arboretum.

You might see us in the yard after lunch, all absorbed by differing visions. Mary sees a bindweed- and wild-geranium-infested garden, patches of snapdragons crushed by napping dogs, and delphiniums decimated by snails. Neither dog nor snail will be spared the wrath of her swearing. I look at hedges in desperate need of trimming. They are infiltrated like the Normandy hedgerows with nettles, blackberries, wild plum, and elderberry. Despite the heavy-duty clippers that I wield a bit like a Gallic broadswordsman, I never come away unwounded or without cutting through the electric cord, tripping the main circuit breaker.

My mother seems to have slipped into restful awareness, gazing into the face of rural beauty that brings order to a disorderly life. Or maybe she's just seeing imaginary goats. Awaking from her apparent trance, she suddenly says, "Those are real opium poppies, you know."

"You're kidding." I peer at them in disbelief. "How do you know that?"

"I just know."

"Like the ones in Afghanistan?"

"Yep."

"How'd they get here?"

"Beats me." I notice the garden is full of opium poppies, and my first thought is, Are they legal? Probably not. I've inadvertently stumbled onto small private marijuana plantations in the neighboring woods, but I never imagined that opium would just come to us. When my brother and I were adolescents, my mother had a special dress for when she was called to court for the mischief we got into. It occurs to me that she might be needing a new one.

"What shall we do with them?"

"Well, you can make tea, use the seeds in muffins, or you could collect the tears of latex from the pods."

"How do you know?"

"I just know."

I find out that growing opium poppies is perfectly legal in France, but processing them isn't. I also learn that I could grow peyote legally, something I end up trying, figuring it will take thirty years for the cactus to achieve full psychedelic maturity. I begin to daydream about the great opium-smoking Chinese poets with calligraphy brushes in hand, and about the Navajo shamans discovering alternate realities in the Chihuahuan Desert. It's hard not to be curious, but downers and alternate realities are not as appealing later in life as they are when you're an adolescent with plenty of energy to spare. Later in life, alternative realities are obligatory, like looking in a mirror. Nevertheless, I go to Carlos Castaneda to see if I am missing any peyote-powered wisdom: "The world is incomprehensible. We won't ever understand it; we won't ever unravel its secrets. Thus we must treat the world as it is: a sheer mystery." Shakespeare knew this long before.

It is July when the poppies drop their petals, pale pink with purple centers, leaving gray-green planetary bodies on stems, their own alternative universe in our garden. I go for a run under the blue lofty sky like the one that Prince Andrei, cracked over the head at Austerlitz, stared into and found happiness in perfect nothingness. I pass an open stretch and the free-range chicken farm, and approach a copse that I swear must have a fine alluvium of shotgun pellets from all the autumn hunters who've shot pheasants, partridges, and doves around it.

And then I see it from ten yards away, the soft brown dome above the moss, the prize of our woods. How could that be, from nothingness? I ask myself; I had just jogged past the very spot a day ago. And now this, a perfect wormless cèpe, eight inches across the cap, on the outer bank of a drainage ditch. It's said that lightning makes mushrooms grow, but we've had none. Yet this one grew like lightning, appearing now, early, out of its normal season when the light wanes through leaf fall, and moisture triggers an enormous earthy bloom.

A WILD KITCHEN NOTEBOOK

Recipes

ALL THREE OF US cook at the presbytery, either taking turns or sometimes all at once, getting in each other's way, and our approaches to the kitchen have a way of revealing temperament and personal, even at times eccentric, vision. Mary is methodical, gifted at sauces and slow-simmered stews. My mother is apocalyptic, cooking five different amazing dishes at once while baking a dessert. I'd like to flatter myself by saying I'm adventurous, but hit-and-miss might be the more accurate assessment. Despite our different approaches and individual food fantasies, though, we agree on one thing: most wild foods have a delicate flavor that must be respected and, when possible, enhanced. Food fantasies also often lead to one wild edible complementing another, for example, *terre et mer,* as the French call "turf and surf," the complementarity of ingredients from land and sea.

Because this book considers primarily foraged foods, it naturally focuses on vegetarian or pescetarian cuisine, while seriously cheating with grocery-store products: milk, cheese, eggs, rice, pasta, and spices.

"If you're going to cheat, you might as well add bacon," Mary decides. "Or chicken broth, for that matter."

Admittedly she is right. Lukasz cooked a grassy-tasting chicken underground, and subsequently used it in many of his broths.

"Look, anyone can simply improvise and add meat products," I say. "A recipe is like music. It provides a theme, and whoever is cooking can take it where he or she wants."

My mother chimes in, "All foods come from the wild originally, so what's the difference? Just make it taste good."

She, too, has a point, and has been the most subversive voice in the process. Still, meat and meat products have been left out.

Once a friend said to me that wild foods are boring, and it would be hard to argue with her if you had to subsist on acorns boiled in water with ash and steamed fern roots. Along these lines, the following recipes will do little to serve survivalists and purists out in the wilderness with only a pot and a knife. I find it hard not to admire these hardy individuals who can liberate themselves from ordinary pleasures to find deeper fulfillment and spiritual satisfaction in the woods. In the end, these recipes are mere suggestions for folks who love to experiment with cooking wild, creating dishes based on foods acquired by the shore, in the woods, or behind their houses.

Note: Starters often can serve as main dishes, depending on how generous the helpings are. The recipes throughout are intended to serve four people.

STARTING WILD
LES ENTRÉES SAUVAGES

Oysters Rockefeller with Borage, Nettles, and Watercress

Mary grew up in New Orleans, where the restaurants garner fame through inventive seafood dishes, especially ones based on local oysters (*huîtres,* in French). Oysters Rockefeller, touting the mysterious recipe of Antoine Alciatore and spawning many versions, is probably best known, followed closely by Oysters Bienville. Mr. Alciatore's idea for his restaurant was to use oysters as an alternative to Burgundy snails, in short supply in Louisiana in 1899. Oysters Rockefeller, named for its richness after the wealthiest American of the era, John D. Rockefeller, became the headliner at Antoine's Restaurant in the French Quarter. Today, the menu also features *Huîtres Thermidor, Huîtres Bienville, Huîtres à la Foch,* along with *Escargots à la Bourguignonne, Escargots à la Bordelaise,* and even *Potage Alligator au Sherry.* No one has figured out Antoine's recipe. Spinach was not included in the original version, making it the perfect dish for imaginative improvisation.

24 fresh oysters, juice conserved
rock salt
1 cup borage (or spinach)
1 cup watercress leaves
1 cup nettles
2 shallots, minced
1 garlic clove, minced
½ stick of unsalted butter
¼ teaspoon cayenne or 1 teaspoon Tabasco sauce
1 tablespoon *pastis* or Pernod
ground pepper to taste
½ cup *panko* (Japanese bread crumbs)
½ cup Parmesan cheese, grated

Open the oysters, cutting them free from the upper and lower shells. Carefully pour off their juice through a filter or fine strainer and conserve.

Then place the shucked oysters in a bowl. Wash the deep half of the shells and place them on a bed of rock salt, returning each oyster to a shell.

Boil or steam the greens until soft, and in a blender chop them very fine. Sauté shallots and garlic in butter until the shallots grow translucent; add oyster juice, cayenne, *pastis,* and pepper; and reduce before adding the chopped greens. Spoon the green puree over the oysters and top with *panko* and a sprinkling of Parmesan. Bake for 8–10 minutes; then raise the oven tray to the grill for a few minutes to brown the topping.

Billi Bi

The story recounted in many guides and cookbooks is that Maxine's chef Louis Barthe invented Billi Bi to please the tycoon William B. Leeds, who frequented the restaurant. Chances are that versions of the popular soup have been around for a long time. Craig Claiborne is credited with elevating this soup in the American consciousness, extolling Billi Bi as possibly "the most elegant and delicious soup ever created. It may be served hot or cold." Onions, shallots, wine, and herbs accentuate the delicate flavor of the mussels, and while good healthy mussels work wonderfully, the flavor of freshly harvested mussels off the rocks makes this soup exquisite.

2 pounds mussels, juice conserved
2 yellow onions, chopped
2 shallots, chopped
1 stalk celery, chopped
2 tablespoons butter
1 bay leaf
parsley, finely chopped
thyme
chili paste or cayenne pepper
1/2 cup vegetable stock
1/2 cup dry white wine
black pepper to taste
1 cup cream
1 cup crème fraîche

Wash and debeard mussels just before using them. Some argue, perhaps rightly, against debearding because it kills the mussels, but in any case each mussel should be cleaned and inspected to avoid dead ones that float or ones that are mud-filled. Place them in a pot and sweat them until just open, shell them, and conserve the juice. In another pot, sauté onions, shallots, and celery in the butter until transparent but not browned. Add the bay leaf, parsley, thyme, black pepper, chili paste, vegetable stock, white wine, filtered juice from the mussels, cream, and crème fraîche. Warm, do not boil. Add the shelled mussels and serve with freshly chopped parsley.

Stuart Dischell cooking mussels just harvested from the rocks (Anse du Guesclin, Brittany)

Sea Urchin and Avocado Crostini

Who needed a dishwasher or even dishes in the Middle Ages, when you ate your meals off rock-hard bread softened in wine, oil, or soup? This is the origin of crostini, now made with sliced ciabatta, a flattened Italian version of French baguette. The ciabatta slices are painted with olive oil and baked, grilled, or pan-fried, after which they can be topped with almost anything and it will be delicious. For something inventive and colorful to brighten winter's gray, I tried sea urchin crostini with avocado, kosher salt, and lemon zest.

This same dish can be made with sea figs, found in the shallow waters of the Mediterranean. Like sea urchins, sea figs provide brilliant orange or yellow to crostini, and both convey an essence of iodine that has been described as a sea kiss.

4 sea urchins
1 avocado
8 slices of ciabatta or baguette
1 lemon
4 tablespoons of olive oil
1 teaspoon kosher salt

Turn the sea urchin upside down, so its mouth at the center is facing you. With kitchen scissors, enter via the mouth and snip the shell in an open

Geoff Gilbert with crayfish crostini (Paris)

circle to expose the orange organs for removal. With a spoon, carefully scoop out the orange parts and place them in a bowl. Rinse away any of the dark material that isn't a part of that orange organ structure. Cut eight slices of avocado and eight slices of ciabatta, and prepare a small pile of lemon zest curls. Pour the olive oil in a frying pan at medium heat and turn the ciabatta so that it becomes golden on each side. Don't hesitate to add more olive oil if the bread soaks it up too quickly. Place the fried ciabatta on a serving dish, top with a slice of avocado, portions of urchin, a pinch of zest, several drops of lemon juice, and a few crystals of kosher salt. Serve while still warm with a glass of chilled rosecco.

Escargot with Nettles

The combination of snails and nettles is a classic in Burgundy and not merely because of the abundance of both in everyone's backyard. They are so synergistic that they inspired the great chef Bernard Loiseau to create *Escargot aux Orties* for his three-star restaurant La Côte d'Or in Saulieu.

Loiseau shocked France by committing suicide, some say over the prospect of losing one of his stars.

The misconception persists that snails are simply a rubbery vehicle for butter, garlic, and parsley. However, the European enthusiasm, particularly in Spain, France, and Italy, for land snails goes back through the ages, and when they are prepared carefully they are tender and have a rich, earthy flavor enhanced by cooking them in court bouillon. Escargot appears frequently on the menus of two- and three-star restaurants for a reason. This very simple recipe is a tribute to Bernard Loiseau.

40–50 snails (from a can if you are not able to process them yourself)

Court bouillon
1 onion, chopped
1 carrot, chopped
2 shallots
1 tablespoon dried seaweed
1 bay leaf
½ teaspoon thyme
1 cup dry white wine

2 cups of fresh young nettle leaves
½ teaspoon of salt
a pinch of pepper
3 ounces unsalted butter

Mix all the ingredients for the court bouillon and bring to a simmer for 20 minutes; then add the preprocessed escargots for 5 minutes and remove. Boil nettles for 3 minutes and squeeze dry; place in a blender with salt and pepper. Melt butter, mix in the nettles, and add the escargots. Serve hot.

Smoked Trout and Wild Berries on Cress, Dandelion, and Peppergrass Salad

In its mixing of many wild edibles, this dish falls under what the French might call *sucré salé,* blending berry and fig flavors with trout that retains a bit of saltiness from the curing process. But one could add peppery and smoky to the description because of the selection of wild greens with a little spice and smoked fish. The raspberry and hazelnut dressing helps to merge these otherwise distinct flavors. As startling a combination as this might sound, the salad brings field and stream to the table in a delicious, colorful, and festive fashion.

2 boneless, skinless smoked trout

Salad
½ cup dandelion greens, chopped
½ cup peppergrass (or wild arugula), chopped
½ cup watercress, chopped
½ cup blueberries
½ cup raspberries
4 ripe wild figs, peeled and sliced into small wedges

Dressing
1 tablespoon raspberry vinegar
3 teaspoons hazelnut oil
ground black pepper to taste
a sprinkle of cayenne

Mix chopped greens with more than two-thirds of the dressing. Place the smoked trout on the greens and decorate with the wild berries and sliced figs according to your fancy, around the edges or on the fish. Add the rest of the dressing and serve.

Wild Blueberries, Feta, and Watercress Salad with Toasted Pine Nuts

The brined sheep cheese known as feta, the national cheese of Greece, has existed since antiquity. When we picture him as the sheep's-milk cheesemaker he was, even the *Odyssey*'s otherwise terrifying, people-eating cyclops Polyphemus shows a domestic side. He was probably producing a form of feta. Every summer my mother makes feta and watermelon salad. It's the easiest salad imaginable: one only needs to find a happy balance in the ratio between two ingredients. Mary goes a step further with a variation on a *sucré-salé* classic using feta on watercress and adding wild blueberries and toasted pine nuts.

1 cup watercress
½ cup wild arugula
3 tablespoons extra-virgin olive oil
2 tablespoons white balsamic vinegar oil
a pinch of ground pepper
3 ounces feta cheese
1 cup wild blueberries
¼ cup pine nuts

Prepare a bed of washed greens dressed with olive oil, balsamic vinegar, and pepper. Crumble the feta on top of the greens; sprinkle the blueberries over the cheese. In a small frying pan, brown the pine nuts, being careful not to blacken them. Scatter the pine nuts over the blueberries and feta, and serve.

Wakame Salad with Scallop Ceviche and Wild Onions

In graduate school, I had a Chilean neighbor who would become so excited about whatever he was cooking that he would knock on my door and insist that I try it. One time it was ceviche, and I was so enthusiastic that I asked him to tell me how to make it. It couldn't be simpler—just "cooking" fresh raw fish in lime juice. I've been making it ever since. The trick is not to let the lime overwhelm the favor, so it's important to drain off the citrus liquid the fish has been bathing in. This recipe uses ceviche on top of a mild wakame salad.

Ceviche
1 cup wild bay scallops
juice of 2 limes
ground pepper
1 or 2 (depending on the intensity) hot green chilis, chopped

Salad
¼ cup shiitake mushrooms
1 tablespoon peanut oil
1 cup wakame (sea lettuce), sliced
1 scallion, sliced; and several strands of wild onion grass, chopped
1 tablespoon toasted sesame seeds

Salad dressing
3 tablespoons rice vinegar
1½ tablespoons toasted sesame oil
1 tablespoon soy sauce
1 teaspoon sugar
¼ teaspoon cayenne
1 teaspoon fresh ginger, grated

Place bay scallops in a bowl with squeezed lime juice and ground pepper and put the bowl in the refrigerator for 2 hours. Then remove from the cold, squeeze out any juice, mix in green chilies, and set the scallops aside. Sauté the mushrooms in peanut oil for 3 minutes and set aside. Hydrate the wakame if necessary, squeeze out liquid, and slice it thinly; then mix it in a bowl with the mushrooms. In a small bowl, stir together rice vinegar, sesame oil, soy sauce, sugar, cayenne, and ginger. Stir two-thirds of the salad dressing with the wakame salad and one-third with the scallops. Place the seaweed salad in a serving dish, top with scallops, and add onions and toasted sesame seeds on top.

Meggyleves: Wild Cherry Soup

The first time I had wild cherry soup was in Szeged, Hungary, where a close friend of Mary's made it for us as an appetizer, calling it *meggyleves,* or "sour cherries cold." It had been brutally hot in Szeged, and I could not have imagined a more refreshing dish, given the weather. I was so taken by *meggyleves* that I ordered it the following night at a restaurant, which then served us delicious whole fried zander, making for a memorable dinner. Wild and sour cherries proliferate in France, and most often find their way into confiture and tarts. But over the years we have become increasingly taken with the idea of using fruit in appetizers, and wild cherry soup is especially easy to make. The trick lies in modulating the level of tartness, which can be adjusted by adding sugar for people who prefer their cherry soups sweet.

2 pounds wild cherries
4 cups water
½ cup sugar (according to your sweet tooth)
½ teaspoon salt
2 tablespoons lemon juice
½ teaspoon cinnamon
8 ounces plain yogurt
3 tablespoons crème fraîche
5 leaves of wild mint

Wash and pit the wild cherries. Simmer water in a saucepan with sugar before adding cherries, salt, lemon, and cinnamon. Simmer until cherries are cooked, approximately 20 minutes. If desired, blend most of the cherries in this juice, saving a few on the side to add to the finished soup. In a medium bowl, add 1 cup of the cherry slurry and begin stirring in yogurt and crème fraîche. Then mix together with the rest of the cherry mixture until uniform. Place in the refrigerator until thoroughly chilled, and then serve with sliced mint leaves as a garnish. This recipe also works with canned sour cherries.

WILD WORLD RECIPES
LES PLATS PRINCIPAUX

Wild Mushroom Risotto

Driving from the northern Italian plain into the Dolomite range of striking pink-red mountains in northeast Italy, you experience an extreme shift in landscape and climate. Suddenly the sweltering humidity and flat fields, so conducive to growing rice, give way to the Alps, where even in summer temperatures drop sharply at night. Just to warm up, we ordered rich, creamy risotto with porcini mushrooms at an Italian chalet restaurant, and gradually we understood the dish in a new way, appreciating all its nuances. The special short-grain risotto rice comes from the Po Valley, and, unlike some other varieties of rice, it becomes sticky, releasing starch when broth is slowly added and absorbed. Cooking risotto is a special pleasure when you sauté the rice and hydrate it with your own broth inventions, mixing in whatever ingredients you choose. Both risotto and broths can be adapted to feature a large variety of wild edibles from land or sea.

Topping

2 cloves garlic, minced
2 tablespoons butter
2 tablespoons olive oil
1 pound of fresh cèpes (porcinis) or 2 cups dried
¼ cup parsley, finely chopped
ground pepper
salt to taste

Broth

2 quarts of water
1 onion, chopped
2 carrots, chopped
2 leeks, chopped
2 branches of celery with leaves
½ celery root
3 sprigs parsley
2 cloves garlic
1 teaspoon peppercorns
1 cup dry white wine

Risotto

½ onion, finely chopped
2 tablespoons olive oil
2 tablespoons butter
1½ cup risotto rice
¼ cup white wine
¼ cup Parmesan cheese, grated
¼ cup mushrooms, chopped

In a skillet, sauté garlic with 2 tablespoons butter and olive oil, add mushrooms, and stir until well softened. Stir in parsley and add salt and pepper to taste. Remove ¼ cup of mushrooms for the rice mixture. Reheat the rest before adding to the risotto.

Broth: Pour water in a pot and bring to a boil, then add onion, carrots, leeks, celery, celery root, parsley, garlic, and peppercorns. Add white wine and simmer for at least 1 hour. Using a fine-mesh strainer, filter off the vegetable broth.

Risotto: In a casserole pan, sauté finely chopped onions with oil and butter until translucent. Add rice and stir for several minutes; then add wine and stir at medium heat until the fluid is absorbed. Begin adding broth one ladleful at time, stirring frequently and simmering down the liquid until the mixture is almost dry before adding more. Continue this process until the rice begins to soften (but not too much). Add the 2 tablespoons of butter, Parmesan cheese, and chopped mushrooms, and stir together for 5 minutes. Salt cautiously. Transfer to a serving dish and sprig with some chopped parsley, adding sautéed mushrooms as topping.

Green Summer Soup

This soup makes a verdant centerpiece for lunch or dinner on hot midsummer days. It is delicious served hot in autumn. You can substitute an array of wild edible greens, and when my borage and Italian greens took over the garden, green summer soup became an especially good way to take full advantage of the growing season. The soup also freezes well. I especially like to serve it to friends on the terrace, knowing that they're enjoying our backyard weeds.

1 large onion, chopped
4 tablespoons butter
2 tablespoons tarragon, chopped
2 tablespoons flour
4 cups vegetable stock
1 cup white wine
2 cups celery root, diced
3 cups borage, shredded
2 cups watercress, destemmed
3 cups of young nettles
1 cup cream
1 cup crème fraîche
Salt and pepper to taste
Finely sliced radishes as a garnish

Sauté the onions in the butter until transparent, add tarragon, and stir in flour. Add stock and wine and stir. Add the celery root and simmer until soft. Add borage, watercress, and nettles and cook until wilted. Purée; add cream and crème fraîche. Chill for about 4 hours. Adjust seasoning. Serve with shredded radishes.

Crayfish and Mousseron Timbale

In Louisiana, where crayfish are known as crawdads, the spicy Cajun recipes require downing beers with pals between each step of preparation. In France, where crayfish are called *écrevisses,* a glass or two of wine from the Ardèche might be an appropriate substitute. The Ardèche is the rough region of pure streams and extinct volcanoes where *écrevisses* traditionally partner in dishes with *mousserons,* small, delicate wild mushrooms, also known as fairy-ring mushrooms. For this marriage of savors, river and forest, we experimented with a timbale, a cup that is used to make a cylindrical form over which sauce is poured.

Mary with crayfish (Burgundy)

Timbale

20 (more if small) crayfish
2 tablespoons crab boil (like Old Bay or your own concoction)
1 cup *mousserons* or any delicate wild mushroom
2 tablespoons unsalted butter
2 shallots, minced
¼ cup white wine
2 eggs
1 cup half-and-half (or milk)
2 tablespoons parsley, chopped
Salt and pepper to taste

Sauce

2 tablespoons unsalted butter
1 shallot, minced
1/4 cup white wine
juice of 1 lemon
1 tablespoon lemon zest
½ cup crème fraîche (or cream)
Salt and pepper to taste

Bring a pot of water to a boil, stir in crab-boil seasoning, add crayfish, and simmer until they turn red (about 3 minutes). Remove crayfish, cool, and pick out tail meat, keeping it intact. Sauté mushrooms in butter until soft, remove, then sauté shallots in butter until translucent; add wine and reduce. Beat eggs in a bowl, add half-and-half (or milk), and pour over the shallots, stirring until the mixture thickens, at the end adding parsley, salt, and pepper. Rub butter on the inside of the timbale cups, place even amounts of mushrooms and crayfish tails in each one, and pour in the cream mixture to the brim. Place cups in a *bain marie* (baking dish with water) and place in a preheated 325° oven for 25 minutes.

Sauce: In a saucepan, add 1/4 cup wine and 1 minced shallot and reduce to a few tablespoons. Whisk in butter slowly until melted; then whisk in lemon juice, lemon zest, and crème fraîche; add salt and pepper.

Place a plate over each timbale and then turn it over, removing the cups from the formed crayfish and mushrooms. Filter sauce over each one with a tea strainer and serve.

Abalone with Artichoke Hearts and Parsley Butter Sauce

Because the flavor of abalone is so delicate, my instinct is to have it as sashimi, but not everyone shares my enthusiasm for eating raw gastropods. Abalone, limpets, and snails are all enhanced by butter and parsley. Looking for a mild companion vegetable, I settled on artichoke hearts for a very simple *mer et terre* dish with a hint of garlic and lemon. One can prepare and serve the dish in creative ways, since the nacreous interior of the shell is jewel-like. I have used the artichoke bottoms as cups for the sautéed abalone and nested them in abalone shells. Alternatively, the artichoke hearts can be sliced and the abalone shells used as serving dishes, as sea otters do.

2 precooked artichoke hearts
⅔ pound abalone
  (calamari substitute)
1 clove garlic minced
2 tablespoons butter
2 sprigs parsley, finely chopped
a few grains of ground cayenne
salt and pepper carefully to taste
1 teaspoon lemon juice
sprinkle of crystal salt

Prepare boiled artichoke hearts and cut them into slices. Cut abalone in thin steaks and pound a few times with a cleaver. Rub skillet with garlic and melt the butter. Sauté abalone until golden and then add artichoke slices, parsley, cayenne, and pepper. Stir briefly and serve with lemon sprinkled on top along with salt crystals.

Insect (Shrimp) Tacos with Garlic and Three Peppers

When considering the prospect of eating insects, I thought maybe I could bury them in cheese-and-bean burritos with jalapeño peppers, turn on a DVD about surfing around the world, and hardly know they were there. This is, after all, how we eat most bugs: unawares. But I promised myself to think positively, and the one dish that sounded remotely appealing was a chili pepper taco with maguey worms. Chile peppers have been a staple in Central America since the Aztec empire, but my fishing buddy, William Montgomery, made chili pepper tacos with fresh shrimp at Matagorda, Texas, on a camper stove, and I never forgot it. Bill reported using serrano peppers with bell peppers, garlic, and onions. I wanted to try the same thing, but using *paquillo* peppers, with ancho and chipotle peppers that I miraculously found dried at a specialty food store in Paris. Peppers have their own Richter scale known as Scoville units, for capsaicin intensity. All the peppers incorporated in this dish—except for cayenne, which I used sparingly—rank fairly low in heat, but anchos have a slightly sweet raisin flavor, and smoky chipotles taste rich. The dish is a hybrid of Mesoamerican and Spanish cuisines. If you are really going to try worms or insects, simply fry them quickly in a little oil. I used bamboo worms (caterpillar of a night butterfly), but the Mexicans prefer considerably larger maguey worms. I can't resist guacamole, so I add it to the recipe.

3 ancho peppers
1 chipotle pepper
⅓ cup bottled or steamed prickly pear cactus (optional)
1 avocado, peeled and pitted
1 clove garlic, pressed (for guacamole)
juice of ½ lime
4 tablespoons olive oil, separated
salt and pepper
pinch of cayenne
1 onion, finely chopped
1 clove garlic, minced
1½ cup sliced precooked *paquillo* peppers (roasted and skinned bell-pepper substitute)
2 medium packages of worms or other insects of choice or ½ pound shrimp peeled and deveined
10 corn taco shells
20 sliced pitted black olives
½ cup chopped coriander leaves

Puff up the ancho and chipotle peppers in a skillet until soft; then remove seeds and stems before pureeing them in a blender with the cactus. Moisten the mixture with a little boiled water but retain a thick sauce. In a bowl, use a fork to blend the peeled, pitted avocado, clove of pressed garlic, juice of ½ lime, 1 tablespoon olive oil, salt, pepper, and cayenne to make a guacamole. Sauté the onions with minced garlic in 2 tablespoons of olive oil; add the *paquillo* peppers for 3 minutes. In a separate skillet, sauté the worms or the shrimp in 1 tablespoon of olive oil; lightly salt and pepper, adding a pinch of cayenne. Prepare the taco shells by baking them or frying them until golden. Serve the pepper/onion mixture, the ancho and chipotle sauce, guacamole, worms or shrimp, olives, and chopped coriander in separate bowls so all can enjoy constructing their own tacos.

Wakame and Crab Imperial Roll Wrapped with Wild Herbs

This Vietnamese-inspired *terre et mer* dish accommodates a number of wild edible possibilities, including variations on the seafood, which can be shrimp, sea snails, or sautéed limpets. The salad wrap with herbs contrasts nicely with the fried rolls. Like the worm-and-peppers tacos, this is a community dish and great fun to share with friends, each preparing wraps based on personal inclinations.

Rolls

1 cake of hard tofu, cut into small cubes
¾ cup peanut oil, separated
2 cloves of garlic, minced, separated
½ cup wild or shiitake mushrooms, chopped
⅓ cup sea lettuce or wakame, chopped
1 cup crabmeat, cleaned
1 tablespoon sesame oil with chili
1 tablespoon toasted sesame oil
1 tablespoon soy sauce
1 package of Chinese wonton wrappers
1 egg white, in a bowl

Dipping sauce

2 tablespoons sugar
3 tablespoons lime juice
¼ cup fish sauce
¼ cup water
1 clove of garlic, minced
1 Thai chili pepper (seeds removed), minced
a few shreds of carrot
2 tablespoons rice vinegar

Salad wrap

20 whole lettuce leaves
½ cup scallions or wild onions, sliced
½ cup mint leaves
½ cup coriander, chopped
hoisin sauce served in a bowl

In a wok, stir-fry the tofu with 2 tablespoons of peanut oil; remove and set aside on paper towel to absorb oil. Clean wok and sauté the garlic briefly in 2 more tablespoons of peanut oil; then add mushrooms and continue stir-frying until they soften. Add seaweed and cook for 2 minutes. Remove mixture and clean wok. In 1 tablespoon of peanut oil, gently stir-fry crab or other seafood briefly; mix in tofu and seaweed mushroom mixture. Season with sesame oil with chili, toasted sesame oil, and soy sauce. Stir briefly and remove from heat.

On a cutting board, place a wonton wrapper in a diamond position; add stir-fried mixture to the middle; wrap the bottom corner over the filling followed by the side corners; and with your finger spread some egg white on the remaining corner to seal the roll when closing it. Repeat this process until you have used up the filling.

In a dipping bowl, dissolve sugar in lime juice and then add fish sauce, rice vinegar, water, garlic, chili, and shreds of carrot.

In a clean wok, add ½ cup of peanut oil, heat to fry rolls a few at a time until golden. Remove and drain on paper towels. Serve rolls and lettuce and herbs on a separate platter. Guests then can dab some hoisin on a lettuce leaf, add herbs and a fried roll, wrapping it to dip and eat.

Classic Borage Ravioli

In Liguria, the meadows in the maritime mountains show off fuzzy clouds of diaphanous blue starflowers. While locals use *borragine* (borage) in soups, salads, and side dishes, it remains a local classic in ravioli. Now I find *ravioli di borragine* in fine Paris pasta shops. While comparisons to spinach are made, borage has a different texture and a fresh flavor, as if cucumber were a leaf. I wanted to feature the essence of this herb, often lost in too much cheese or pesto sauces that overwhelm it. Here it's presented in a simple butter sauce.

Filling

4 cups borage, chopped
1 shallot, finely minced
3 tablespoons olive oil
1 tablespoon Parmesan cheese, grated
4 tablespoons ricotta
salt and pepper to taste
a few shavings of nutmeg

Pasta
1½ cups softest flour (00 Italian)
2 eggs
½ teaspoon salt

Sauce
4 tablespoons butter
salt and pepper to taste
a few shavings of nutmeg
grated Parmesan to taste
borage starflowers for decoration

Put the borage in a pot of boiling water for one minute, drain, and squeeze out water. Chop finely in blender. Sauté the minced shallots briefly in olive oil at medium heat before adding the borage; mix well while sautéing for 2 minutes. Add the Parmesan and ricotta and continue to sauté for a few more minutes to solidify the mixture. Add salt and pepper to taste and shavings of nutmeg sparingly.

Mix flour, eggs, and salt by hand or using a processor until dough is formed. Knead until the dough is smooth and silky. Roll the pasta dough very thin on a flour-coated board; place soup spoonfuls of filling in mounds on one-half of the thin dough and ring them with water. Then fold the dough over the mounds of filling, pressing around them with your fingers to seal the ravioli. Use the lip end of a glass to cut through the dough; then pinch the ravioli edges to further seal them. Knead together the dough and repeat the process.

Boil a large pot of water, add pasta and cook until tender (approximately 5–8 minutes). Drain and add butter, salt, pepper, and nutmeg. Top with grated Parmesan cheese and beautiful starflowers from the borage.

Wild Mushroom Quiche

I must have been seven or eight when my mother taught me how to make quiche. It's one of the simplest dishes to prepare since it includes a master ratio of 1½ cups of cream or milk to 3 eggs that can be applied to dessert custards. The fun part is that practically any wild edible can be added—wild asparagus, spicy greens, mushrooms, or seafood—as long as they do not exceed half of the filling's volume. These can be baked in a precooked pie shell, or in no shell at all, or baked in timbales.

Pastry
2 cups flour
¼ teaspoon salt
¼ pound butter
about 4 tablespoons water

Put flour and salt in a processor. Add the butter, cut up into small pieces, and process 10 seconds until mixture looks like coarse cornmeal. Add water and process until pastry forms a ball, no more than 15 seconds. Wrap the pastry ball, refrigerate for 1 hour, and then roll out the pastry.

Custard
3 eggs
1½ cups light cream
½ teaspoon salt and freshly ground pepper

Filling
3 shallots, finely diced
1½ cups mixed wild mushrooms, coarsely chopped
1 clove garlic, finely diced
4 tablespoons butter
⅓ cup parsley, finely chopped

For the custard base, beat eggs in a bowl and then beat in light cream with salt and pepper. Sauté shallots in the butter until transparent; add mushrooms, garlic, and parsley and sauté until lightly browned; taste for seasoning. Add to custard. Line the quiche dish with the rolled-out pastry, add the custard mixture, and bake in a 375° oven for about 1 hour, or until a knife comes out clean.

Classic Linguine Alle Vongole in Bianco

Clams are alchemists. How do these creatures transform marsh muck into mild clear juice and sweet pinkish bodies? No one was more clam crazy than the Indian tribes who spent summers on the shoreline near where I grew up in Connecticut. Clams might be even more adaptable in cuisine than oysters, finding themselves stuffed, swimming with potatoes in chowder, or sitting on top of pizzas consorting with bacon. One doesn't have to search far in clam cuisine to find an Italian classic: *linguine alle vongole in bianco.* A variety of clams can be used for this dish, even the tiny coquina. Cooking clams briefly in their own juice is the key to this zuppa-like dish, and just a teaspoon of minced fresh red chili transforms it into a timeless culinary treat. Some cooks like to add a little wine, but I'm more of a purist.

2 pounds littleneck clams
(or carpet clams in England)
12 ounces linguine
3 tablespoons olive oil
2 cloves garlic, minced
1 fresh red-hot chili pepper
(seeds removed), minced
½ cup parsley, chopped
black pepper to taste
(no salt!)

Place clams in a basin of water for ½ hour. Rub each clam between your fingers, making sure it's still alive and not filled with mud or sand. Start a large pot boiling for the pasta and add linguine before cooking the clams. Sauté garlic briefly in olive oil, add chili pepper, then clams and cover, and raise heat. The clams will steam themselves open within 3 minutes. Be careful not to overcook them, or they will toughen. Drain linguine and place in a bowl, mix in a little olive oil. Once the clams have opened, add chopped parsley and black pepper, and pour clams and juice over the linguine. Serve with an extra bowl for clamshells.

Dragon Roll with Nori and Sesame Scales

Even for the weird sisters in *Macbeth,* tracking down dragon scales for their brew must have been difficult. Today, with Internet shopping, you can acquire exotic ingredients more easily, though "scale of dragon" remains a challenge. For wild edibles, I have turned to a Japanese classic, the dragon roll, made with barbecued eel and nori seaweed. In the wetland channels and estuaries near Marennes, famous for its oysters, eels and shrimp can be netted at the same time. If it seems like a lot of trouble filleting and barbecuing your own, you can purchase frozen barbecued eel at your Asian market.

½ cup sushi rice
2 tablespoons rice vinegar
1 teaspoons sugar
¼ teaspoon salt
1 barbecued eel
4 sheets nori
2 tablespoons toasted sesame seeds
4 avocado slices in strips
4 cucumber slices in long, thin strips
1 teaspoon wasabi
slices of red pepper for decoration
2 tablespoons soy sauce

Follow directions on the box for cooking special sushi rice. Remove to a bowl. In a small saucepan, heat rice vinegar and add and melt sugar and salt. When translucent, remove from the heat and slowly pour small amounts of the vinegar mixture into the rice while chopping and mixing it in.

Place the eel on a metal sheet with foil and grill it in the oven until the surface bubbles and darkens. Remove and slice free one full-length half. This will be the dragon's back. Slice the rest into long strips for the filling.

The nori sheet will end up with a rice coating on the outside and a filling on the inside. Place a sheet of roasted nori on a cutting board, and, after wetting your hands, press down a thin blanket of sushi rice over the surface and sprinkle with sesame seeds. Cover with a sheet of plastic wrap and carefully reverse it on a sushi rolling mat. Through the middle of the nori, add a thin line of wasabi. Along the line place what will become the filling: strips of cucumber, avocado, and barbecued eel, keeping in mind that you will need space to roll around the filling. Dampen the upper edge of the nori and roll it tightly with the mat while compressing it. Remove plastic wrap and place eel on top along the length of the dragon's body, cutting the remainder of the eel for topping a second roll. Secure the eel with bands of nori, which can be cut to look like scales. With a very sharp knife, cut sushi segments between the bands and arrange in a serpentine shape on a platter. Repeat with a second roll. The head, whiskers, wings, tail, and dragon fire can be created in imaginative ways to make it your own dragon.

Start this true food-art dish with the basic rolls and the natural serpentine shape of barbecued eel. After that, begin playing with the food, making a head out of a lemon, avocado, or cucumber. Find colorful vegetables to make wings, feet, scales, and fire. The professionals use bright, multicolored sauces on the plate and run lines through them with a knife to create a blazing dragon effect.

Navajas (Razor Clams) with Green Salsa

Two of the great specialties of Gallica, Spain, are gooseneck barnacles (*los percebes*) and razor clams (*navajas*). Anyone who has tried and appreciated the flavor of gooseneck barnacles is hard-pressed to describe it. The closest I can come is a very tender version of a steamer clam neck or the delicate muscle parts of a razor clam. And certainly just a butter dip with a hint of lemon suits all.

Razor clams always presented a challenge when I'd dig for them as kid. They have a remarkable ability to elude predators by creating a kind of quicksand and literally sucking themselves more than two feet down. Seagulls tend to outsmart them, listening and then plucking them out of the sand the way robins nab worms. Over the years, I have come to appreciate razor clams as one of the most delicious seafoods in Asian, Spanish, or French cuisine. I chose two versions of razor clams based on a Mesoamerican-Spanish mix—one fried and one sautéed.

Jalapeño Salsa (to be used sparingly)

1 clove garlic
1 onion
1 tablespoon olive oil
6 pickled jalapeño peppers (seeds removed), chopped
3 tablespoons preserved tender cactus (optional)
½ cup coriander, chopped
juice of 1 lime

Sautéed in Garlic

2 pounds of razor clams
4 cloves garlic, minced
¼ cup red pepper, diced
¼ cup olive oil
¼ cup white wine
¼ cup coriander, chopped
salt and pepper to taste

Panko-Fried Razor Clams

2 pounds razor clams
½ cup *panko*
½ cup peanut oil
salt and pepper to taste

Start with salsa preparation by sautéing garlic and onion in olive oil until soft. Add jalapeño peppers and cactus, stirring for a minute. Place the mixture in a blender, adding coriander and lime juice, and grind to make a slurry. Add water if the mixture is too dry. Pepper and salt to taste.

To prepare clams for either dish, simply use a sharp knife to slice them on the open side of their shell, remove them, and cut away all organs but the neck and muscle.

For the razor clams and garlic dish, sauté garlic and peppers in olive oil. When the peppers are soft, add wine and reduce by half; add clams for one minute; add coriander, salt, and pepper. On a platter or plates, arrange shells and return clams to them, pour sauce over them, and serve with jalapeño salsa.

For the fried version, season *panko* with salt and pepper and spread on a plate. There's no need to dip the clams in milk or egg; simply roll them in the seasoned *panko* and fry them in a skillet with peanut oil. Remove and drain on a paper towel. Serve with jalapeño salsa. The Spanish would have them with aioli sauce (garlic mayonnaise.)

Mussels in Saffron on Brown Rice

I spent a good part of my youth eating brown rice. It was a part of the kind of macrobiotic diet in which everything, it seemed, had to taste bland in order to be healthful and planet-friendly. Brown rice was among my favorite foods in those days, at least compared with the brick-like bread we had to eat. Mostly, I think, my parents were trying to feed the family on very little money.

Later in life, I came to appreciate what is called brown rice, or, more appealingly, *riz complet,* complete rice in French. Here I've mixed it with wild mussels and saffron, which has always fascinated me because it comes from the autumn crocus, one of my favorite flowers.

1 cup whole-grain rice
3 pounds mussels
½ onion, finely chopped
1 clove garlic, minced
2 tablespoons butter
½ cup white wine
½ teaspoon powdered saffron
¼ teaspoon salt
¼ teaspoon ground pepper
½ cup cream
3 tablespoons parsley, chopped

Prepare whole-grain rice according to the directions on the package. Steam open well-washed mussels, being careful to avoid overcooking. Remove the mussels from their shells and place them in a bowl. Sauté onion and garlic in butter on medium heat until transparent. Add wine and reduce until most of the liquid has evaporated. Mix in mussels, saffron, salt, and pepper and stir for 1 minute before adding cream. Prepare a bed of rice or four separate servings of rice, top with mussels and saffron, sprinkle with chopped parsley, and serve.

Seaweed Soup with Wild Mushrooms, Cockles, and Black Cod

Fish soups exist in a huge range of preparations, and from vastly different traditions. In France one thinks immediately of bouillabaisse, a rich fish stew originating in Marseille but available throughout the country. The story goes that it's the invention of a fisherman's wife's who wanted to make use of catch that would not sell.

There are also bisques and *fumés* that make use of the heads, bones, and shells of fish and crustaceans. One is Normandy's *marmite dieppoise,* exceptional because it blends the delicate flavors of fish and shellfish in the soup and at the same time maintains the integrity of each ingredient, none of which is overcooked or masked by tomato, for example. In the spirit of showcasing the fish ingredients and seaweed, I opt for a very simple, clear soup. To make it, I use a wonton soup base. Most people would probably make a chicken stock base with low salt content, but a vegetable stock would work just as well. I use fresh black cod or pollock because it retains its texture and flavor in broth.

½ pound cockles
6 cups vegetable broth
1 clove garlic, minced
1 tablespoon ginger, grated
1 cup wakame (sea lettuce)
1 cup sliced wild mushrooms (or shiitake)
½ cup enoki mushrooms
1 scallion, sliced
1 pound black cod filet, sliced into cubes

Steam cockles and deshell them. Bring the pot of broth with garlic and ginger to a low boil; add seaweed, mushrooms, and fish and simmer for 5 minutes. Add scallions and cockles and simmer another minute and serve.

Omelette aux Herbes

The first wild edibles dish I had in Poland was nettles and herbs mixed with eggs, not so far from the French classic *omelette aux herbes.* Cooking in Italy with leftover ingredients, we couldn't resist our own variation on this ancient dish. I imagine that over the millennia, people have gathered eggs from all sorts of birds, domestic and wild, and cooked them with whatever ingredients were at hand. Here in the twenty-first century, we combined the French *omelette aux herbes* with the classic Italian combination of ricotta and a touch of Parmesan. We served it with sliced tomatoes and toasted Ligurian foccacia.

For this recipe, we made four individual omelettes, each using one-quarter of the ingredients.

8 eggs, room temperature
¼ cup milk
2 tablespoons nettles, finely chopped
2 tablespoons borage, finely chopped
pinch of salt and pepper
4 ounces ricotta cheese
2 tablespoons wild onion or chives, chopped
2 tablespoons Parmesan cheese, grated
4 tablespoons butter

Beat eggs in a bowl with milk, nettles, borage, salt, and pepper. In a separate bowl, mix ricotta, chives, and Parmesan. In an 8-inch skillet, melt at a medium heat enough butter to coat the bottom; pour in ¼ of the egg mixture to cover the bottom. Once the eggs begin to stiffen, add ¼ of the cheese mixture to the center and cover it to let steam melt the filling. When the eggs are almost cooked, use a spatula to fold the omelette in half and slide onto a warmed dish. Repeat to serve four.

"WILD SIDE" DISHES

Wild Asparagus Etouffé au Jus de Truffe Noire

This recipe for one of the most delicious of all vegetables incorporating the essence of truffles uses a process of cooking vegetables by surrounding them with butter plus a few tablespoons of water in a hermetic environment over very gentle heat. *Etouffé* literally means smothered. The asparagus releases its own juice and is cooked in it, so none of the taste is lost. Much of the success of this method of cooking is in the sound: the vegetables should never dry out too much or cook too fast. The addition of *jus de truffe* is not essential to the recipe, but the truffle juice synergistically enhances the taste of the original ingredients, butter and asparagus.

¼ lb wild asparagus
2 tablespoons butter (very fresh)
salt and pepper to taste
1 tiny can of *jus de truffe noire*
(this is a water-soluble extract
of black truffle)

Trim the asparagus. You want to keep as much of the stem as you can, but it quickly becomes fibrous below the head elements. Use the knife to judge where the tender part ends.

Melt a generous glob of butter over slow heat. Add the asparagus and permit it to sizzle very gently for a few minutes in the butter, until all stalks are well coated. Cover the pan with a tight-fitting lid.

After 2 or 3 minutes, check to make sure that the butter is not browning. If necessary, reduce the heat or use a damper; add salt and pepper to taste plus 1 or 2 tablespoons of water or a little can of *jus de truffe noire.* Cover again. After 5 minutes, check the asparagus for doneness by squeezing with the edge of a fork tine; if it has softened, it is ready. You want the asparagus, when served in a soup bowl, to swim in a small amount of liquid. If necessary, reduce the liquid or add water to have 1 or 2 tablespoons of liquid per serving. Serve with a fork and a teaspoon to permit tasting of the pure juice.

Pommes de Terre en Bateau avec Champignons et Oignons Sauvages

This recipe takes a baked potato and transforms it into a cargo boat for the essence of the forest: wild mushrooms. You can use any type of wild mushroom, including morels, chanterelles, hedgehog mushrooms, cèpes, or a combination of them. If your dog happens to dig up a truffle for you, a special version of the potato boat can be devised, featuring two subterranean gifts. This recipe can also be adapted for wild greens and herbs.

2 large Idaho baking potatoes
3 tablespoons olive oil, separated
2 tablespoons shallots, minced
2 cloves garlic, pressed
1 cup wild mushrooms, roughly sliced
2 tablespoons wild onion (or chives), chopped
salt and pepper to taste
2 tablespoons *panko*
2 tablespoons Parmesan, grated
4 tablespoons butter

Bake the two potatoes. When they are done, cut them in half lengthwise and scoop out much of the inner potato flesh, conserving it in a bowl and leaving the skins as self-supporting shells. Fork butter into the potato flesh while it is still hot to make a puree. In a skillet, heat half the olive oil and sauté shallots until translucent. Remove them cleanly and set on a side plate. Then heat the rest of the olive oil and add mushrooms, tilting the pan if necessary to evaporate liquid. Add the sautéed shallots and pressed garlic and cook briefly. Then add mushroom mixture to the bowl with the removed potato and mix the ingredients, mashing them with a fork. Add wild onion and salt and pepper to taste. Return mixture to the potato skin shells and top with *panko* mixed with grated Parmesan. Bake again for 10–15 minutes and finish under the grill until the top is golden brown.

Seaweed and Mushroom Salad

I grew up at the seashore without knowing that you could simply pluck seaweed from the rocks and eat it. Of course, this would not be quite the pleasurable experience that eating seaweed salad is. Most seaweed salads are very plain, using mainly sliced-up wakame and a simple Japanese dressing, but far more elaborate versions can be developed that include fried tofu or bean threads.

½ cup wild or shiitake mushrooms, sliced
1 tablespoon peanut oil
1 cup sliced wakame (sea lettuce)
½ cup sliced thongweed
½ sliced dulse
½ cup saltwort (optional)
1 small carrot, grated
1 scallion, diced (or several strands of
  onion grass, chopped)
3 tablespoons rice vinegar
1½ tablespoons toasted sesame oil
1 tablespoon soy sauce
1 teaspoon sugar
¼ teaspoon cayenne
1 teaspoon ginger, grated
2 tablespoons toasted sesame seeds

Sauté mushrooms in peanut oil until softened. Transfer mushrooms to a salad bowl and mix with the sliced seaweeds, saltwort, grated carrots, and scallion. In a separate bowl, mix together rice vinegar, sesame oil, soy sauce, sugar, cayenne, and grated ginger, then pour over the seaweed mixture and sprinkle with toasted sesame seeds.

Wild Greens in Golden Triangles

One August, we ferried our car from Marseilles to Tunis and drove through much of Tunisia, finding ourselves in Tozeur in 110-degree heat, wine bottles in our trunk uncorking themselves and our car reeking. Tozeur is where the great Sahara sand dunes begin to the south. To the east lies the Chott el Djerid, a lake known for its Fata Morgana—superior mirages. Our whole midday experience felt hallucinogenic until evening came and temperatures approached the bearable. At dinner we had a Tunisian specialty called *brik,* a savory pastry containing vegetables and cheese, accompanied by lemon, olives, and *harissa.*

I planned to try making a garden-weeds version of spanakopita, but Mary said, "Why not try *brik*?" In France, you can buy thin sheets of *brik* pastry in almost any grocery store, and even in November in our backyard the freshest nettles, dandelions, and borage grow. We went about inventing.

1 cup young nettle leaves
1 cup young dandelion leaves
1 cup borage leaves
½ onion, finely chopped
1 clove garlic, minced
3 tablespoons olive oil
½ cup feta cheese
½ cup ricotta cheese
1 tablespoon olive paste
salt (if necessary)
½ teaspoon pepper
a few shavings of nutmeg
6 sheets of *brik* pastry
1 egg white
3 tablespoons butter

Bring a pot of water to a boil and add nettles, dandelions, and borage. Cook for 3 minutes. Drain the greens, squeezing out excess liquid, and then grind them finely in a processor. In a skillet, sauté the onions and garlic in olive oil to soften, then mix in greens. After a minute or two, stir in feta and ricotta and cook mixture a few minutes until firm. Add olive paste, pepper, nutmeg, and salt (if necessary).

Slice *brik* pastry sheets into triangular quarters. On each triangle, place filling in a small mound of the vegetable mixture. Spread egg white along the edges of each pastry and seal it, rolling edges as necessary. Melt the butter with the olive oil, and then paint each triangle with the mixture. Fry until golden in a skillet with just a little olive oil. Serve with lemon, *harissa,* and olives.

Onion Grass and Pine Nut Sarma with Borage Yogurt

Ever since I tasted Lukasz Luczaj's delicious colt's foot *sarmas* in Poland, I wanted to try something similar. *Sarma* means rolled food, most often in a cabbage or grape leaf. While most Armenian and Turkish recipes call for lamb or other types of meat, some use just a few simple ingredients with herbs.

½ cup whole-grain rice
¼ cup pine nuts
5 tablespoons olive oil, separated
1 small onion, finely chopped
1 clove garlic, minced
¼ cup wild onion, chopped
¼ cup parsley, chopped
2 tablespoons wild dill, chopped
2 tablespoons wild mint (optional)
salt and pepper to taste
pinch of cayenne
juice of 2 limes
16 grape leaves
1 cup yogurt
1 cup young borage leaves

Prepare whole-grain rice according to package instructions. Toast pine nuts in a skillet and set aside. Sauté onions and garlic in 2 tablespoons of olive oil until soft; mix in rice and stir. Add pine nuts, wild onions, parsley, wild dill, mint, salt, pepper, and a pinch of cayenne. Add lime juice and stir for 2 minutes to solidify the mixture. Wash grape leaves and add filling to the center of the leaf, allowing enough leaf around the edges to wrap them tightly. When all the rolls are ready, heat 3 tablespoons of olive oil in a skillet and fry the rolls until brownish. In a separate bowl, mix yogurt with chopped borage leaves and a squeeze of lime. Salt and pepper to taste and serve as a topping or dip for the *sarma* rolls.

WILD FINISH

Blackberry Flummery

One of Mary's fond memories of her childhood visits to Highlands, North Carolina, is of the blackberry flummery her stepmother would make. This dish, well known to the English, Welsh, and Irish, is perfectly suited to the Great Smokies, where blackberries abound. At home in Burgundy, the dragons I cannot slay are hedges of coiled blackberry brambles, so I feel they owe me their abundant gifts.

1 quart of blackberries
1 tablespoon lemon zest
½ cup sugar
2 tablespoons cornstarch
3 tablespoons water
juice of ½ lemon

Cook berries and lemon zest with ½ cup of water and sugar. Bring to a boil, stirring frequently, and cook for 5–7 minutes. Strain the cooked berries, pushing the pulp against the wire to collect everything except the seeds. Return the juice to a cooking pan, dissolve the cornstarch in 3 tablespoons of water, and add it slowly to the fruit while stirring. Add juice of ½ lemon, bring again to a slow boil, and cook for 1 minute. Pour into little dessert bowls. Eat warm with cream or chill in refrigerator and serve with cream or yogurt or nothing.

Wild Berry Panna Cotta

Here is a recipe to show off your wild berries when you are trying to convince friends that wild edibles are fun. Leave it to the Italians to invent a kind of Jello made with cream. The only mistake you can make with this dish is to let the mixture boil, or even simmer.

2 cups wild berries
2 cups heavy cream
2–4 tablespoons sugar, depending on the sweetness of the fruit
1 teaspoon powdered gelatin
2–3 tablespoons water

In a saucepan, combine berries, cream, and sugar. Heat slowly and stir until steam begins to appear. *Do not simmer or boil.* Remove from heat and allow to cool, then pour the warm liquid into a wire strainer. Using a wooden spoon, stir and press the macerated fruit against the mesh to push as much of the pulp through as possible. The longer you do this, the more intense the flavor will be. Soften the gelatin in cold water and mix it into the liquid slurry and heat again while stirring until steam appears. Pour into ramekins and place in the refrigerator for several hours to allow gelatin to set.

Wild Fruit Zabiaone

While *zabiaone* originated in Italy and is classically associated with Marsala wine, it is a widely celebrated dessert to finish summer or winter feasts or for major holidays in Europe and North and South America. Each country makes its own cultural contribution to the recipe, usually in the form of a regional alcohol. It is served as soft topping, a custard, or even a sweet drink. *Zabiaone* is related to eggnog, the Trojan Horse of all drinks, often masking enough hard liquor to produce a major hangover.

1 cup of wild berries or fruit
1 teaspoon lemon juice
1 teaspoon sugar
3 egg yolks
¼ cup of Marsala wine
¼ cup powdered sugar

Place berries or fruit in a bowl and mix with lemon juice and 1 teaspoon of sugar. Whisk together egg yolks and 1/4 cup powdered sugar; then, in a small bowl heated in a double boiler, whisk in the wine little by little. The key to *zabiaone* is to whip air into the mixture like whipped cream, but thicker, while keeping the yolks from turning into scrambled eggs. Serve warm or cold with wild fruit or berries. For a baked version, place berries in small baking cups and pour the prepared *zabiaone* mixture over the berries until they are covered. Place the cups under the broiler for only a couple of minutes, watching to make sure that the top or mixture doesn't overcook. The idea is to serve the baked *zabiaone* as a custard.

Wild Strawberry Surprise

Wild strawberries grow in our old stone staircases, gardens, and all through the orchard. They smell like perfume. This recipe is a special strawberry surprise (maybe sacrilege) for your guests, whether you use wild or raised ones. It is fun to ask your guests to guess what is in the dish: they are rarely able to do so correctly.

1 quart of strawberries
  (or as many wild strawberries as you can get)
2 tablespoons of lemon juice
dash of sugar
olive oil (just enough to coat them)
ground black pepper

Gather as many strawberries as you can. The wild ones are small, so you'll need a bunch. Clean them and let them sit in some lemon juice with a dash of sugar. Place the berries in little bowls and add a teaspoon of olive oil per bowl. Grind a little pepper on top.

Beignets d'Acacia avec Fraises de Bois

The acacia flowers that find their way into French and Italian cuisine in fact come from black locust trees. In spring, the grapelike white blooms seem ubiquitous in Burgundy. At the same time, you can find wild strawberries. Chef Danièle Mazet-Delpeuch first served us acacia fritters, as Americans know them. We were taking a course with her in the Dordogne on different duck preparations, during one of which she had us taste raw liver out of a freshly butchered duck. We experienced a number of memorable firsts during our apprenticeship. Madame Delpeuch went on to become the personal chef of former French president François Mitterrand and the subject of a major film.

My mother often serves flowers with meals, but primarily for the flair they add. But black locust flowers play a starring role in this dessert with wild strawberries, adding color and perfume. My mother says to shake the insects out of flowers before cooking them, but that's up to you.

Olivia Baes admiring wild strawberries, mint, and acacia flowers (Rogny-les-Sept-Écluses, Burgundy)

1 cup flour
1 teaspoon baking powder
1 tablespoon powdered sugar
½ teaspoon cardamom
1 egg
½ cup ice water
½ cup cold milk
1 quart peanut oil
3 cups of acacia flowers

Mix together the flour, baking powder, sugar, and cardamom. Separately, mix together the egg, milk, and ice water. Then, lightly mix the egg mixture with the flour mixture; a few little lumps are okay. Keep batter cold. The flowers should be dry before being dipped into batter and fried in hot, deep oil until crisp. Remove excess oil from the flowers on paper towels, transfer to plate, and put with wild fruit of any kind, here with wild strawberries in season, and sprinkle with powdered sugar.

Brandied Wild Cherries on Pound Cake

Spring is the most impressive season in France. The flowering fruit trees, wild and renegade, fill the woods and line the country roads. It's as if the country were dressed up, the first to flower being the wild plum trees and then the wild cherries, the blossoms bright white with yellow stamens droning with bees. The wild cherries come in midsummer, bright red turning to purple. They taste refreshingly tart. We've preserved them in brandy because they make a great complement to desserts, especially pound cake. Pound cake in France is known as *quatre-quarts* for its four equal parts of flour, sugar, butter, and eggs.

Brandied wild cherries
1 quart wild cherries, pitted
2 cups brandy (your choice)
sugar to taste

Pound cake
2 cups flour
½ teaspoon salt
1 teaspoon baking powder
½ pound butter (2 sticks)
1½ cup sugar
4 large eggs
½ cup milk
1 tablespoon kirsch (or brandy)
1 teaspoon vanilla
1½ teaspoon lemon zest

For the topping, collect wild cherries, rinse and pit them. Place cherries in a glass canning jar with a tight-fitting top and add the brandy of your choice to cover. Allow them to sit for at least 2 months, the longer the better. When you wish to use them, add sugar to taste.

Sift together flour, salt, and baking powder. In a deep bowl, cream together the butter and sugar. Add the eggs one at a time, incorporating each with beating. Then alternate the addition of the milk and the flour mixture, ending with the kirsch, lemon zest, and vanilla. Line a greased loaf pan with bakery paper, add the cake dough, and knock the filled pan against the table to distribute the dough evenly and bring up air bubbles. Bake at 350° for about an hour: it is ready when a knife blade plunged into the cake comes out clean. Serve cake sliced on dessert plates with brandied cherries spooned on top.

Wolf's Tooth Cookies

After our winter trip, we returned to Liguria in better weather, but this time we stayed in Santa Margherita after taking the boat out there instead of Sestri Levante. Locals in the area are crazy about two things: dogs and sweets. Every other person on the walkways is attached to at least one dog and may at the same time be eating an ice cream. We fit right in with our dogs greeting our friendly neighbors.

Santa Margherita has a far higher concentration of *gelatarie* and *pasticcerie* (ice cream and pastry shops) within four blocks than *coiffures* and *pharmacies* in Paris. Granted, Paris has endless *chocolateries,* and the French will stand up to the world with their pastry. But in Italy, even the croissants are sweet, and every imaginable pastry form is cream- and chocolate-filled and sugar-powdered. Also Italy has the very best pine nuts, stone pines towering along the coasts, and I think the first pine nuts I can remember were in my mother's crescent almond cookies. If you remove half the crescent, then you have a wolf's tooth cookie.

8 ounces almond paste
½ cup sugar
½ cup powdered sugar
¼ cup flour
2 egg whites
8 ounces pine nuts

In a food processor, break up almond paste, add 1/2 cup of sugar and flour, and mix. Add egg white and mix until dough forms. Wet your hands and scoop up some dough to form into a wolf's tooth. Roll in pine nuts. Bake on baking paper at 300° until golden. Top with powdered sugar.

Index of Recipes

Acknowledgments

This book is a gathering of personal experiences, cooking experiments, scientific and anecdotal information, and cultural references all related to wild edibles. While I already had much personal experience gathering limited kinds of wild edibles when I started this project, I was for the most part a neophyte in the broader subject of foraging and the culinary preparation of wild edibles. Driven by curiosity, I have taken the reader on my journey of discovery. I consulted a wide range of sources that included articles, guidebooks, cookbooks, and literary works. Still, more important to me are the people who contributed to the story and the preparation of this text: Jean-Pierre Campagne, Lukasz Luczaj, Laurent and Catherine Harvey, Roger Ramon, Corine Thuilier-Delahaie, Gereon de Leeuw, Susan Prospere, Madame Diégues, Stuart Dischell, Dan Gunn, Geoff Gilbert, Olivia Baes, and Chauncey Alan. This book would not have been written without the enthusiasm, good humor, and tireless editing of Boyd Zenner, acquiring editor at the University of Virginia Press. Copy editor Susan Murray has been an angel on my shoulder for two books now. I am also extremely grateful to Jason Coleman, Ellen Satrom, and Emily Grandstaff at the Press for strongly encouraging me and working closely with me on this project. My greatest thanks go to my mother, Gretchen Van Blaricom, whose wild spirit and wisdom appear in one form or another on every page. Finally, I would like to thank literary agent Laura Strachan for her friendship and abiding support. Research funds from the American University of Paris are deeply appreciated.

Sources

Borgarino, Didier, and Christian Hurtado. *Le guide des champignons.* Aix-en-Provence: Édisud, 2004.

Calvino, Italo. *Marcovaldo, or The Seasons in the City.* Translated by William Weaver. London: Vintage, 1983.

Erichsen-Brown, Charlotte. *Medicinal and Other Uses of North American Plants.* New York: Dover, 1979.

"Field Guide to Economically Important Seaweeds." www.noamkelp.com/technical/handbook.html.

Fischer, David W., and Alan E. Bessette. *Edible Wild Mushrooms of North America: A Field-to-Kitchen Guide.* Austin: University of Texas Press, 1992.

Fleischhauer, Steffen Guido, Jürgen Guthmann, and Roland Spiegelberger. *Plantes sauvage comestibles.* Paris: Ulmer, 2012.

Génevé, Alain, and Marie-Jeanne Génevé. *Baies et fruits sauvages de France métropolitaine.* Paris: Rouergue, 2013.

"Give Thanks for . . . Eel?" www.nytimes.com/2010/11/25/opinion/25prosek.html?_r=1&.

"Gooseneck Barnacles Feeding and Growth." www.asnails odyssey.com/LEARNABOUT/GOOSE/goosFeed.php.

"Growing Pine Nuts: Unlocking the Food." www.youtube. com/watch?v=BvpV4Ox2HN8.

Guillemard, Colette. *Les carnet des cuisininières.* Paris: Berger-Levrault, 1983.

Hazan, Marcella. *Essentials of Classic Italian Cooking.* New York: Knopf, 1992.

Heaney, Seamus. *Field Work.* New York: Farrar, Straus and Giroux Classics, 2009.

"How 'Magic Mushroom' Chemical Could Free the Mind of Depression, Addiction." http://edition.cnn.com/2014/09/17/health/magic-mushroom-chemical-depression/index.html?hpt=hp_c6.

"L'huître pied de cheval, un met rare et délicat." http://videos.tf1.fr/jt–13h/2009/l-huitre-pied-de-cheval-un-met-rare-et-delicat-5583249.html.

"Last Chance Foods: The Unexpected History of Eels." www.wnyc.org/story/163366-last-chance-foods-unexpected-history-eels/.

"Lightning Makes Mushrooms Multiply." http://news.nationalgeographic.com/news/2010/04/100409-lightning-mushrooms-japan-harvest/.

Luczaj, Lukasz. *Dzikie rosliny jadalne polski.* Krosno: Chemigrafia, 2004.

Mabey, Richard. *Food for Free.* London: Collins, 2012.

McMichael, George L. *Anthology of American Literature.* 2nd ed. New York: Macmillan, 1980
Melville, Herman. *Moby-Dick.* New York: Wadsworth, 1999.
"Oyster Nutrient Content: A Mineral-Rich, Depression-Fighting Food." www.rebuild-from-depression.com/blog/2010/03/oyster_nutrient_content.html.
"The Oysters of France." www.oysters.us/france-main.html.
Pepin, Jacques. *The Art of Cooking.* New York: Knopf, 1987.
Perkins, David. *English Romantic Writers.* New York: Harcourt, Brace, and World, 1967.
Pivot, Bernard. *Six grands cuisiniers de Bourgogne.* Paris: Jean Claude Lattès, 1982.
"Plants for the Future." www.pfaf.org/user/cmspage.aspx?pageid=37.
"The Seaweed Site." www.seaweed.ie.
Shakespeare. *The Riverside Shakespeare.* Boston: Houghton Mifflin, 1974.
"South African Pastor Makes Members Eat Grass." www.christianpost.com/news/south-african-pastor-makes-members-eat-grass-watch-him-command-demon-out-of-womans-stomach–112320/.
"Taste of the Wild." www.bio.brandeis.edu/fieldbio/Edible_Plants_Ramer_Silver_Weizmann/Pages/Growthtype.html.
Vicomte de Mauduit. *They Can't Ration These.* London: Persephone, 2004.
Williams, William Carlos. *Collected Later Poems.* New York: New Directions, 1963.
Wright, John. *Edible Seashore.* New York: Bloomsbury, 2010.